Boer Goats

Boer Goats: facts and information.

Raising, breeding, housing, milking, training, diet, daily care and health all included.

by George Hoppendale

Table of Contents

Table of Contents

Table of Contents

Foreword

Growing up with animals, I have learnt so much about taking care of them. The most amazing thing about pets is the fact that they are so unconditional and so grateful for every small act of kindness. It is rather humbling to see how warm-hearted animals can actually be.

I would have never had the wonderful opportunity of dealing with goats and other animals if it had not been for my family, especially my father.

I have always watched people in my home interact comfortably and affectionately with animals. So I extend a heartfelt thank you to every single person in my home that taught me the right way to care for animals.

My father always kept me around animals. I guess he was trying to help me learn how to be tolerant and loving from these amazing creatures. Trust me, some of the biggest life lessons that I have gained have come from these beautiful creatures.

My family, too, has always been hands on with the pets in the household. Animals were the centre of all our activities. There was not a single day that did not begin with a discussion about our pets. What to feed them? What is the most nutritious thing to feed them? These were common dinner table conversations while I was growing up. So, needless to say, I have had a lot of practical training regarding taking care of different breeds of animals. Sometimes, I learnt from my family and sometimes, your pet will just tell you what he or she needs. Today, I am in a very privileged place where I can share this information with pet lovers across the globe.

I would have never been able to write books with so much comprehensive information without the knowledge that I gained from my father, my family and of course my beloved pets.

Introduction

As robust, exotic and unique animals, Boer goats are fantastic animals, not only as dairy and meat animals, but also as pets. Adaptable and hardy, Boer goats can be kept by almost anyone with enough knowledge and time. Because of their good temperaments and easygoing nature, they make great pets, with some owners even walking them on leads like dogs.

Boer goats are increasingly popular pets as people are learning what great animals they are to have around. People keep Boers as they are sweet natured and an excellent option if you want to have a couple of milkers at the same time but *don't* want masses and masses of milk, or for people who want to make their own goats' milk products, such as cheese, yoghurt, butter and non food items like soap. This is because, although Boers don't produce anywhere near as much milk as dairy breads, the milk they produce is far higher in milk solids.

Boer goats are very good producers for their type, though, producing up to 2 litres a day at the peek of their season. The milk is sweet and thick, with high butterfat content.
Boers are just as disease resistant as other goats if they are bred well, and have excellent health in general. They are hardy and cute. There are lots of fantastic reasons for having Boer goats, but

if you want to get the most out of a dairy animal, a Boer is still the best bet.

Boer goats are great animals to keep, either as pets, companion animals or as an alternative dairy option. They are both entertaining and very useful. They do fantastic work keeping the lawn cropped, as they browse and don't clip the grass too short, and keeping other animals company. They produce good quality, high butterfat milk without having to be bred from every year. And they gambol about happily being all too cute for words!

The main draws of the Boer goat are their even, predictable temperament, their ability to rub along well with other types of animals and their robust, strong bodies.

While the milk is good quality, with Boers, the milk tends to dry off more quickly, within about 5 months. This can actually be very handy if you don't want a full time farming commitment and many goat owners say Boers are great if you ever want to go on holiday and have a non-farming neighbour look in and feed, as if you go away after goats have dried up they don't need to be milked twice a day. This means that you don't have to worry about asking for quite such a big favour from your goat sitter.

A Boer goat is also a fantastic addition to an existing herd, being strong and of good temperament and they have a cheering influence on their peers and herd mates, remaining youthful and exuberant well into old age. They also make a good basis to cross from and have a good, wide gene pool, being bred predominantly in South Africa by the Dutch.

They are also an excellent addition to the bloodlines of any crosses you might want to breed, having strong lines and a good management history. Adult Boer does (over 18 months) make fantastic mothers, and can be relied upon to raise big, strong kids.

The decision to keep any animal is a big one and you need to be informed. You kneed to know about any special housing requirements. You need to know what they eat and if they need any dietary additions. You need to know about any potential breeding complications. You need to know the benefits of owning them too, and there are so many pros; it's not just a missive list of cons.

What you need at this stage of the game is get information. This book will tell you all you need to know in order to make the rest of this decision.

Chapter 1) Boer goats

Traditionally having been bred for meat by the Dutch white farmers in South Africa from African and northern European breeds, the Boer is recognised as having very high quality, if low yield, milk. Boer goats are incredibly well mannered and easygoing if they're reared properly. As with all animals, hand raised individuals are often precocious and can be pushy if they're allowed to be, so you can't let your little bucklings and doelings push you about, even when they're little and cute, as this can grow into a bad habit.

Boers have a bit of a bad reputation as bad mothers, as bad feeders and as bullies. This isn't specific to Boers and is certainly something I've ever come across.
Bad mothers in the Boer population are usually does who have been bred too young and don't really know what to do. The first time a doe freshens (has a kid and comes into milk) she should really have older does about to help keep her calm, and should be over a year old.
Boers that haven't been used to pasture from a very young age can be fussy about eating grass. If you get your Boer from a

breeder who keeps them on pasture then they will be much more likely to feed well on yours. Goats of any kind that grew up on pellets aren't going to know to rummage and forage properly to get the best bits of eating from your land. This isn't just a Boer trait, but it can be avoided. By choosing a non-commercial breeder, or a free range breeder who has kept the goats in pasture where they have had to forage properly, you can make sure your goat won't be too fussy.

The reputation for being bullies is completely un-earned. Some Boers can be bullies, just as you can get bullies in any breed. In general, they get on well with other animals, even timid animals or animals that have physical problems. As long as you aren't trying to keep intact males with wethers or kids you shouldn't have problems. There can be issues when you keep bucks together as they fight for dominance and respect.

The physical characteristics of the Boer are rather varied when it comes to colours and markings, despite the popular miss conception that they are only red and white. They can be red and white paint – white with red rump and face, dappled cream shades, blond, black, chocolate, full red, traditional white with a red face and they can have all manner of patterns. In fact, Boers that don't have the stereotypical red face and white body markings have usually been bred for health and stamina rather than colourings, and will often be in better long-term health. If you are looking for show Boers, though, you need the traditional colouring. This is white with red on the head, neck and front of the shoulders, with little to no red elsewhere. The coat will be short as they are African in origin and the kids may well need some protection from cold weather in the form of a coat.

Most Boers available from hobby breeders or pet homes will be some sort of high percentage cross, and will have various other colours, which is fine for most pet or hobby owners and is an indication of a wider gene pool, which is an indicator of good general health.

The size, shape and weight are quite specific, with the weight being very important. A healthy adult male Boer should be between 240lbs and 360bls, with does coming in at a much smaller 150lbs to 260lbs. Boers are considered fully grown at 3 years old.

The Boer has a large, low body. They have fat backsides and strong, meaty legs. A good Boar goat will have a slight look of a body builder about them, with a convex Roman nose and a muscular, bulging chest.

They really do look like the meatheads of the goat world, with their long breeding for a large, high quality meat yield, although they are quite sweet in temperament.

Because of the prominent Roman nose, Boers are often mistaken for the other proboscis prominent breeds like the Nubian. These breeds also have long, floppy ears and a tendency towards reds, browns and whites. The way to tell them apart is firstly the general shape – Boars are stockier and taller than Nubians and secondly the meaty neck. Boers – especially males – have a very distinctive, short, meaty neck, usually with a ripped, well-defined musculature.

Both male and female Boers have horns. The male's horns are longer and more robust than those of the female. The barrel (tummy) may be slightly less well developed than the female. Boers can have 2, 4 or occasionally 5/6 teats. This isn't very useful, as the udders only have 2 chambers, so only 1 pair of teats needs to be milked. Sometimes there will be 4 fully functioning teats, which can be helpful for triplets or quads, but usually only 1 pair works and the others are under formed and not functional at all.

Wethers are somewhat more sturdily built than females, but not obese. They do not develop the typical male head, neck and shoulders, though they will still have short, muscular necks. The horn growth is usually less than in the entire male. They make fantastic pets, tending to a very sweet nature and a friendly disposition. They make fantastic companions for does and kids, as they don't try to boss or dominate them, but will provide the herd the safety that they need.

Goats are such clever beasts; it's quite amusing to watch as they learn. Once shown the proper way of doing something, for example being let out of their pen to be milked and where to stand, a Boer will soon learn to walk to the right place on their own, clamber up and wait to be milked. Being full of milk can be quite uncomfortable and they will soon know that the people and the milking help it to feel better, and make them feel comfortable again.

Both males and females have a medium-long coat, and one of its most attractive features is the variety in colour. Many coat colours are permissible within the breed; white caramel, medium caramel, dark caramel, dark caramel (red), silver-light grey agouti, medium grey agouti, dark grey agouti, black with frosted points, and solid black. Many colour combinations are found, which give some very pretty mottled, marbled and tortoiseshell animals.
You'll find the most common colouring of Boers to be white, with a red head or face. This is because most Boer goats have been bred for this colouring in the past, though now more emphasis is on the general robustness of the breed than on the look.

No two Boer goats are the same, not even twins or real siblings. Each Boer goat has a distinct personality and each one will have specifically distinct needs. While most Boer goats will be friendly, not all will be delighted to see you. Not all will welcome you home like a faithful pet dog and not all will be delightfully pleasant companions. However, most are congenial and docile and more often than not, their happy days will far outnumber the crabby ones.

Even with the gender, females are generally docile and good-natured, while the males are a little more stubborn, obstinate and independent. Boer goats sure know their minds and you could say they stubbornly stick to them. Boer goats hate getting wet so to prove my point, try getting one outside when it is raining. He is sure to dig in his heels and give you a tough time, for someone so tiny. It is a breed that really mellows with age and there are many examples of healthy females breeding successfully and milking well even at 10 or 11 years old. Many animals of the type are productive and renowned for their fertility. Twins, triplets or quadruplets can be very common among Boers when the dam is well managed.

The Boer goat is one of the largest and heaviest breeds of goat. The males have a longer, thicker and wirier coat than is found in the females and tend even more to be overweight.

Males will show the same upright standing position and variety in colour as the females, though first time goat owners generally only have females, or perhaps females with a male kid at foot. This breed does really well with heat, as they originated in West Africa. This means that they're a great source of food in the third world, and their high milk yield for their small size and lower food intake means that they can provide protein long-term.

Due to their strong genes, calm temperament and growing availability all over the world, the Boer goat is increasingly successful. It has been successfully crossed with native goats of most countries to raise either the milk yield or meat production, or both.

Milk production is very good, producing 1.5-2.5 litres of milk per day with the correct nutrition at the height of their milking season, although they don't milk anywhere near as long as other breeds at 5 -7 months before drying off. Many Boer owners see the short milking periods as a real advantage on hobby farms and smallholdings. As meat animals, the milk is designed for fast kid growth and so has a very high concentration of milk solids, making their milk ideal for cheeses and other value added milk products.

Nubians
The Nubian goat is one of the heaviest and tallest breeds of goat, being almost as big as the Boer, with males weighing up to 140Kgs and females to 110Kgs. The males have a longer, thicker and wirier coat than is found in the females. They also have a more convex nose than the females, much more 'sticky-outy'. Males will show the same upright standing position and variety in colour as the females.

This breed does really well with heat, like the Boer, as they originated in North Africa. This means that they're a great source of food in the third world, and their high milk yield means they can provide protein long-term too.

It has been successfully crossed with native goats of most countries to raise either the milk yield or meat production, or both.

Pygmy

Pygmy goats are incredibly popular pets and have a fantastic way about them. People keep pygmies as they are smaller and more compact, but still have a cheeky outlook that you'd expect from a goat. They are really sweet and an excellent option if you have limited space or want to have a couple of milkers at the same time but *don't* want masses and masses of milk.

Pygmy goats are very good producers for their size, producing up to 2 litres a day at the peek of their season. The milk is sweet and thick.
Pygmies are very disease resistant and have excellent health in general. They are hardy and cute.

Guernsey
The golden, beautiful, longhaired, cream or pale red Guernsey goat is a fantastic goat for those who don't have masses of land but want to produce milk. They are much smaller than typical dairy breads, but still have a good yield, producing about 3-4 litres a day in the height of their season. The Guernsey is the sweetest natured of all the goats and has a lovely disposition with most other animals and children. They are much smaller than the Boer, standing at 75-85cm or 29-33 inches tall.
There are 2 breeds of Guernsey, the Golden Guernsey from the Bailiwick of Guernsey in the Channel Islands, and the British Guernsey, though the two types are very similar, with the British Guernsey having high concentrations of Golden Guernsey in their line.

Toggenburg
The little Swiss Toggenburg is a lovely animal, sweet natured and yielding high milk for their size. Toggenburg goats are smaller than the Boer with good, strong muscling. The colour can range from mid-brown to shades of grey or fawn, with white Swiss markings. They are stocky, with little legs and have long, proud necks. The head is distinct, being wide across the level of the eyes, and having a dished face like the Pygmy. The hair can be any length, but is usually long and fringed. The Toggenburg is a good milker for their size, giving about 3 and a half to 4 and a half litres per day at the height of their season.

Saanen

The Saanen goat is a very good milk producer, averaging at a very high yield, and although their butterfat is lower, there is more milk produced. This makes the Saanen a great goat for producing drinking milk, but not so good for cheeses, butters and yoghurt.

They are very beautiful to look at too, having lovely pale blond to white hair, big, inquisitive eyes, and short, proportionate legs. Saanens have shorter, pointier ears than the Boers, and while the ears aren't as cute, they are more practical for cleaning and grooming purposes.

Saanen goats are better suited to the cold than the shorthaired Boer, which needs to be kept warm in winter, as they originate in cooler, northern climes. This makes them well suited to northern Europe and the northern United states.

Boer-Pygmy

The Boer-Pygmy cross is a sweet little cross, with a longer milking season than the Boer and the milk is thicker than that of the Pygmy. If you are crossing a Boer and Pygmy, or buying a cross, you need to the male to be Pygmy and the female to be Boer, otherwise there is a huge risk for the dam, both in carrying and in kidding. This cross has some beautiful markings, and makes some truly lovely little kids. There is something comical in the round bellies and little legs of these animals.

Boer-Guernsey

These are a truly beautiful cross, with a real grace about them. The Boer-Guernsey is a much hardier breed and more tolerant to the colder northern climates than the Boer is, although they still need protecting from the elements. They have the strength and vigour of both breeds, the strong, muscular bodies of the Boer, the long hair of the Guernsey and they stand a little smaller than the Boer. The are very good milkers, giving 3 litres a day in the height of their season, with the season sometimes being as long as 8 months.

17

Boer-Toggenburg
The Boer crosses well with the smaller Toggenburg. They tend to have a slightly dished nose compared to the Boer, but they have quite a straight face. They produce well, but only for 5-7 months. Like the Boer-Guernsey, the Boer Toggenburg is a much hardier breed and more tolerant to the colder, northern climates than the Boer is, though, like the Boer-Guernsey, they still need protecting from the elements.

Boer-Saanen
Saanen goats are quieter and can have a slightly higher yield than Boers, and the cross Saanen-Boer is a fantastic cross, though often much daintier in frame than the Boers, with similar milk production. This cross can usually produce milk for 6-8 months, though not always.
The main benefit of the Boer Saanen cross is the temperament and adaptability. They are also cheaper to buy than pedigrees.

1. Health benefits of Goats

There have been ideas for years that pets are good for your health. Stroking a cat or dog has a soothing effect and the responsibility of pet ownership has a generally stabilizing effect on mood and behavior. Studies have shown that owning a pet can increase the levels of endorphins in the brain and can increase physical health, improve sleep patterns and stave off illness. Pets can reduce the symptoms of depression. The soothing, repetitive action of stroking a pet has been proven to lower blood pressure.

How do Boer goats fit in with this?
Because of the closeness of the bond between a Boer goat and their owner, the love and affection shown can seriously improve one's mood.
If you find yourself becoming isolated, pets, especially less common ones, are really good icebreakers. By joining an owners'

forum and going to meetings and shows you can find that you
have a network of friends across the world.

Pets can really push you to social interaction in ways that you are
never going to be negatively judged. Owning an animal can be a
great and unusual thing to have in common with people, and
joining forums and going to goat shows with people can help you
to make connections with people in low pressure environments.
The depth of the bond between a Boer goat and it's owners means
that they make great companion animals.

It's strange, but even when you struggle to take care of yourself
emotionally, having a dependant who relies on you to get out of
bed and feed and cuddle "can help give you a sense of your own
value and importance", according to Dr Ian Cook, director of the
Depression Research (UCLA).

The uncomplicated nature of the bond between a Boer goat and
their owner can be a great antidote to complex family and social
relationships.

Having a routine with your Boer goat can add structure to your
day and this is a fantastic way to keep your mental health on
track. Milking needs make you get up. The needs of others can be
really good for you, and goats of all types need to be milked every
morning. Having to get up in the morning can massively improve
your mental health. It is excellent relaxation therapy that helps
you develop an extra special bond with your milking does.
Getting to the goat shed to milk twice daily enhances your
management of both the goats and things in your own life; you
notice details and tend to keep up with things a little better. You
are more likely to spend time outdoors in the fresh air, which is
good for your mental health, as well as your physical health.

Recent studies show that children raised with animals, even little
house pets, are more confident, happier, healthier and do better at
school than children who aren't raised with animals.

The confidence that comes from having animals around grows out of the comfort and nurturing that animals foster in children. 40% of children studied reported that they look for their animals when they are upset.

The health benefits of animals are well documented. By the age of six, some children reduce their chances of getting hay fever or an allergic reaction to house dust mites by 75 per cent. Pet owners in general require fewer doctor's visits.

They also have higher educational attainments due to their higher motivation, which comes from the confidence and the responsibility they get from keeping pets.

There are also lots of health benefits to switching from cows milk to goats milk, as, although it has a higher fat content, the fat is more digestible than that of cows milk.

Goat milk has more of the essential vitamins that we need. Goat milk has 13% more calcium, 25% percent more B6, 47% percent more vitamin A, and 27% more selenium. It also has more chloride, copper, manganese, potassium, and niacin than cow milk. It also produces more silicon and fluorine than any other dairy animal. Silicon and fluorine can help prevent diabetes. Scientist are not sure why, but people who are lactose intolerant can often drink goat's milk without having to worry about side effects. Goat's milk does not cause phlegm like cow milk does, so you can drink goat's milk even when you have a cold or bad allergy problems.

There are also a lot of benefits to drinking fresh milk over pasteurized, as a lot of the vitamins and minerals are damaged during the pasteurization process. It also makes a lot of the calcium in milk difficult to absorb, while at the same time making the sugars more easily absorbed. This means that pasteurized milk not only doesn't give us all the calcium that we think it does, but it doesn't let the body feel full for as long as it should.

Milk, produced in the home, is generally not going to be pasteurized, but heat treated. Heat treated milk is far better for you. A cow will generally produce too much for a single family, but goats are just right.

There are a few questions you need to ask, though. A Boer goat can live for up to 15 years and they need constant attention.

2. How many?

Goats need to live in a herd, but the herd doesn't need to be a traditional herd of goats. It is cruel to keep a goat on it's own and they will quickly become unwell. A lonely goat may even stop producing milk. You don't need a whole herd of them, other animals will do. They can live in any herd type, with sheep, or ideally Boers or other goats. They can't really cope on their own and need companionship.

3. Can you afford it?

They can be very costly, not just in the initial outlay on the animal itself but the feeding and housing requirements also need to be taken into consideration. As well as this, you may need to pay out for medical expenses (vet bills, medicine and travel to and from the vets if they're not close).

Will you be available to clean the housing out often enough? You need to clean them out completely and change all of their bedding and litter every week, including making sure their toys are clean. You'll also need to do a spot clean every day, taking out any obvious soiling and wet bedding.

4. Do you have enough space for a goat?

Even these diminutive little guys need a large amount of space to move about in. Just because they are smaller than other livestock does not mean that they can be kept in a small yard. They need access to grazing, as well as a space they can be kept away from ground that is too lush. They also need access to somewhere indoors where they can be out of the weather, such as a shed, barn or even a stable.

5. Can you make the commitment to milk them twice a day?

Goats need to be milked twice a day in order to keep them in milk. They need to be milked twice a day to be comfortable too. It's not fair to leave them without milking them and this can cause all sorts of medical and behavioural problems. *Can you cope* with a grumpy/huffy goat and keep up the daily handing and fussing to get them back to their sweet old self? If your goat is a dairy goat, she will need you to continue to milk her twice daily, even if she stops liking you or you fall out.

Failure to make reasonable efforts to keep animals in your care comfortable, in this case failure to milk goats is against the animal welfare acts in the USA, the UK, New Zeeland, Australia and most mainland European countries. The need for twice daily milking while they are in milk is one reason for keeping Boers, as they do not produce milk all year round.

6. What would you do if they bit you?

Could you cope with the idea that your lovely, cute baby has hurt you on purpose? While the bite may not be vindictive, it can really hurt your feelings when something you have nurtured and loved breaks the trust and snaps at you. While unlikely, all animals can bite, and a Boer bite can be quite nasty, as they are big, chunky animals. If this happens you need to be able to pull yourself together and get on with making your Boer safe again. This can only happen if you remain calm and collected. Being in control of yourself can be hard if your pet distresses you.

7. Can you meet their dietary requirements?

They need grain, access to pasture and a varied diet of vegetables and leaves. They need a constant supply of fresh water, too.

8. The downside

There is a downside to every story, and there are difficulties with Boer goats – with any goats.

Boers don't produce milk all year round. While a lot of Boer owners use this to their advantage – taking the opportunity to go on holiday/ visit family – this can be a real problem if you are milking for any sort of retail purposes. In the southern United States and Australia you can re-breed your Boers to make them freshen again, but in the UK and northern United states – anywhere cold, really, they will only breed in the spring.

They are noisy, and although happy Boers are usually much quieter than a lot of other goats, the slightest disturbance can set them off at all hours. You need to be aware of any neighbours you might have. If they live close to your house and they aren't deaf you need to really think about how fair it would be on them to keep goats.

They can smell terrible. Seriously, an ill or badly kept goat can smell like week old unwashed socks. If you keep them clean, then there shouldn't be a problem, but if you don't you'll need a strong stomach.

They need tending to every day. Your whole life changes when you have livestock. You can't just nip over and stay with family at Christmas without making provisions for the goat to be milked. This makes any kind of social life or holiday plans very hard.

Ask any goat owner though- they'll tell you it's all worth it.

Chapter 2) Goats in the wild

Genetic tests indicate that all domestic goats are descended from the wild Bezoar Ibex of Anatolian Zagros, (a part of the Middle East.) Scientists still that believe goats are one of the earliest domesticated animals, with evidence that suggests they were domesticated at least 10,000 years ago.
Goats are incredibly adaptable creatures and can survive very well in the wild. They are fantastic browsers and can find food almost anywhere. They can be a pest in places, as they will strip the bark off trees like deer if they can't find enough grass feed.

When we think of goats in the wild though, we always think first of mountain goats. With their distinctive, sharp horns and beautiful short, white coat, they are very striking to look at. They have strong, broad shoulders and strong legs. The tail is short and the snout is long and straight.
Mountain goats aren't biologically goats, but they are, for all intents and purposes, goats. They look like goats. They move like goats. They behave like goats and apparently taste like goats. They can climb steep accents that even the most well equipped human climbers would balk at.

24

They are so well suited for climbing steep, rocky slopes with pitches exceeding 60°, with inner pads that provide traction and cloven hooves that spread about to make the hold stronger. They even have dewclaws like dogs and cats have, to stabilise them. They can jump up to 12 feet in one go. The males are very aggressive towards one another. The mpost common cause of death among mountain goats is murder. They knock each other off their purchase and push each other down cliffs. Male mountain goats will almost all fall to their death at the hands, or horns, of another goat.

Both males and females have beards, short tails, and long, black horns. The males are very tall, standing at about a meter, and are about 30% heavier than the females, making violent encounters very dangerous.

Mountain goats are real tough customers. When they're in the wild, goats will live in large herds, for both protection and companionship. There can be as many as 500 does and kids in a herd. Males will tend to be solitary, avoiding each other wherever possible, and only joining with the females when they are in oestrus.

Any large predator will see goats as potential prey, and depending on where they live there can be some very frightening things out there in the dark. This accounts for the need to be nimble and fast. Males will often fight very aggressively and in breeding season these conflicts can occasionally lead to injury or death, but are usually harmless. To avoid fighting, an animal may show a posture of nonaggression by stretching low to the ground.

The females will generally only fight to protect themselves and their young. And they can fight ferociously. Nanny goats have been known to take out cougars, lions and wolves, though bears are a different story.

Because of their amazing adaptability and tolerance for change, goats are found all over the world.

Most of the goats found wandering about in the wild tend not to be true wild goats, but feral populations of domesticated goats. There are true wild goats, such as mountain goats etc, but the majority of 'wild' goats are feral.

A lot of country parks and native animal reserves will have a section for wild goats. There will be a wild grassy area with boulders and goats.

The problem with the success of goats is that when they become feral, they become a problem. Goats adapt really well. Environments don't adapt so well to goats, though.

Goats are excellent at finding food. They can strip entire grasslands and trees. They can kill trees, devastate crops and decimate native grazing populations by eating all the food.

Chapter 3) Choosing your goat

So you're getting yourself a Boer goat or two. You need a healthy one. Getting a sick goat is bad for you and the goat, so don't do it. To avoid getting an ill goat, look for general signs of health.
The goat should be alert and lively, and it should move easily, without limping or acting stiff or sore. It should have firm, pellet poo. Be sure it has no abscesses, and of course you'll want a well-shaped udder and teats on a milking doe. Check the feet for muck and splits. The abdomen should be firm but not hard and the goat should not flinch or show discomfort at touch.
Before you get your goat, make friends with some friendly goat owners on one of the forums. These people are knowledgeable and usually closer than you may think. They will be able to advise you on goats for sale near you, and may even accompany you to help check out your prospective new goat if you ask nicely.
Of course, you won't bring a goat home until it has a place to stay and something to eat.

1. Where to get goats

Choosing where to get your goat can be as important as choosing the Boer itself. The main thing to consider is what you want from your animal. The information in this part of the book is fairly general, and you'll be able to find more specific information on where to get your goat locally to you from local goat owners. I strongly recommend joining forums and other online communities to get advice and support on specific things local to you.

a) Auctions

Livestock auctions are not for the faint hearted. If you choose to go down this root with your first goat, it is a good idea to have someone with you who knows about them. If you're friendly with a vet that would be ideal, but if not, try to make friends with a goat owner local to you, or from one of the forums. Buying a goat at auction has a lot of risks associated with it and you really shouldn't consider this as for a first goat.

Most auction animals are from big herds or are otherwise destined for the dinner table. This means that they could have all manner of health and psychological problems that would not have been picked up on.

b) Breeders

There are all sorts of arguments in favour of getting your goat from a breeder. Breeders often have lots of advice and will usually offer excellent aftercare. Local breeders will be able to advise you on things like feed suppliers, veterinary services and other owners local to you. Boers born in captivity are better adjusted to life in captivity. Being able to trace the lineage of a Boer will mean that you can avoid any congenital diseases.

Professional breeders

Professional breeders are often breeding for industrial scale agriculture, but they will usually sell to the general public. Because of the high turnover of animals, though, you shouldn't expect personal attention or masses of after sales care, though they will have fantastically detailed advice for you that you should pay attention to if you do choose to go down this root.

Pet owner / hobby breeders

Hobby breeders or goat owners will often have great quality kids available. They will tend to have a lot more time for you and will be generally be very attached to the animals they are selling. If you get a goat kid from a local Boer goat owner who has a spare, then you will also have someone with good knowledge of the breed and a vested interest in the health of your animal, who lives not too far from you. Even though Boers are sometimes only kept as pets, and not bred for milking, most owners will breed from their Boers so that they produce milk and will be happy to find someone else to look after and to love the kids. Pet and hobby breeders will more likely have crosses available than full breed Boers. This is often a good indicator of long-term health and longevity.

2. Choosing your goat

If this is your first goat and you're getting them as a milker, you should really get a doe with a kid at foot. This means that your goat will be producing milk and you don't have to deal with the breeding or the kidding or any of that scary stuff before you get to know your goat. It also means that your goat won't be alone, as they need company. In addition, you won't have any of the problems of introducing unfamiliar animals to each other. A male kid at foot can be castrated when he is 8 to 12 weeks old to make a friendly, happy wether to keep his mum company in the long run and a female kid can be used to breed from in turns so that you don't end up with one exhausted, constantly bred doe.

Look at the parents. The mother goat should be strong and have a good udder, with a slight upwards dip between the teats (medial suspensory), not too much, and not with them hanging down, as this can mean the udder will eventually be damaged and this can be genetic. Look for a goat with 2 teats. This makes them easier to milk and more likely to produce kids with only 2 teats. This is also better if you intend to show.
DO NOT COLLECT A KID UNDER THE AGE OF 12 WEEKS. They are too young to leave mum and no responsible breeder will let them go this early unless mum has aggression issues.
If you intend to keep her as a pet for a while before you breed and milk her, you should get a few female kids or a female and a couple of wether (castrated male) kids and spend time getting them to trust and care for you. They should be perky and bright eyed.

The stance should be strong, with the legs straight up from the ground – leaning forwards, backwards or to the side can be a sign of illness.
They should be happy and healthy. They should bounce about and have a lot of energy and sparkle.
The feet should be clean and free from any cracks or overgrowth. They should point straight forwards.

The elbows should be neat and straight, not bandy and all over the place. The goat should stand over the front feet rather than between them. Tight elbows mean the front of the goat will be stronger and generally in better health.

The back legs should be a bit bandy, though. The part where the udder is attached, at the top of the groin, is called the escugheon. This should be nice and wide, as this is where the udder will swell with milk, and a wide escutcheon makes for an easier life for your goat.

The chest should come out in front of the legs a little. A little bump is a sign of general strength and vitality. The line from the neck to the knees should not be straight in a healthy, well-formed animal.

The withers (shoulders to you and me) should be higher than the bottom and hips. This is known as being up hill. The more up hill the better.

Young does frequently look like fawns rather than goats; very slim through the body, and while it's pretty, it's not correct. They should be quite stocky looking, as you'd expect of an adult.

Chapter 4) Caring for your goat

Goats are herd animals, so should not be kept as solitary animals. A pair (or preferably more) of goats will make a good addition to the right family. A decent amount of space (yard/pasture) will be necessary, depending on the breed and number of goats, so they are best suited for rural areas on farms or acreages. If you live in a city, bylaws may prevent you from keeping goats as they will likely be classed as an agricultural species.

You must also be prepared for the commitment to having goats. They do need attention like any other pet, and you need to consider who can look after the goats if you must go away, or if something should happen that means you cannot keep the goats.

1. Housing and pasture

Goats are hardy animals, but they do need a dry, draft-free place to sleep and to escape from the hot sun or rain, and an outdoor space to exercise. If you get a few goats it's probably worth having a field shelter as well as a shed.

My neighbour keeps pygmies in his goat shed next to his house. Note the kidding shed next to it in the same fenced off area. In terms of housing, this set up (or something similar) would work well for Boers too, as they are both from warm climates and while the Boer is much bigger, they don't need masses more indoor space – they'll be playing out most of the time anyway, right?

The ground around the shed is tarmac, meaning that less mud and mess is brought in to the bedding from outside in the fields.

The proximity of this shed to his home means that it gets residual heat from the house, the brick wall behind the shed also heats up at the say time and releases heat during the day. It is shaded from too much heat, but is south facing so that things that heat up can get very warm to release more heat at night time. This is

important, even with such robust animals as Boer goats, as they don't have a lot of long fur – being South African in origin, and can cool down quicker than hairier breeds.

Another bonus of having the goat shed so near the house is that goat owners can hear anything untoward. Boer goats are generally quite vocal, (though some aren't) and will make a lot of noise if anything is wrong.

One important thing to think about when considering your shed is that although your goat doesn't need a lot of height, cleaning out will be a lot easier if you can stand up in the shed. Having something full height will make your life a lot easier. It's also a good idea to have the shed fenced off from the grazing, as you can muck out in winter without having to find them again, and you can let keep them somewhere while waiting for vets etc but they won't feel trapped indoors.

In hot areas where protection from the sun is important, a simple roof or lean-to might suffice. In a colder climate, you'll need to protect your animal from the cold, the wind, the driving rain and all of the other horrid things we have to contend with. Here a shed is a must, and your goat will need to be able to get out of the weather when they are in the field too.

Most goat raisers recommend anywhere from 12 to 25 square feet of shelter per animal, the lower figure being adequate in warmer climates where they will spend more time outdoors. In cold or wet areas, the goats will often be fed indoors and will spend more time there, increasing the space requirement.

Outdoor spaces are equally flexible. You might need little more than a small exercise yard for few goats. Or you might want a pasture area that will provide at least some of the goats' nutritional needs. Lots of people choose to section off the pasture areas so that they can rotate and rest the pasture, getting the most out of your land.

The number of animals you can keep on the land depends on the amount of space you have, the types of plants that grow there, and the food supplements and grain you will be giving. They need to be able to move about freely and to graze on land that is clear of their waste. Being able to separate off areas of pasture and to rotate it is a real boon for avoiding parasites such as worms.

The space needed is another advantage of goats over cows, as you can raise more goats on a smaller amount of pasture than you can cows. While it takes an acre per a cow/calf, you can successfully raise six goats on one acre.

They are also more efficient milk producers than cows; pound for pound a good dairy goat will produce more milk than a cow will. Unlike a cow, a good dairy goat can produce up to 10% of it's body weight in milk.

Tethering

Tethering is not advised unless absolutely necessary, and is illegal in parts of Australia and New Zealand. This is a technique for tying an animal out to graze on a rope. The rope is staked to the ground and the stake can be moved about as the land is grazed. Goats can be tethered with a radius or about 5 metres. If you do tether your goat you need to make sure they always have access to water and that you are supervising them – if the weather turns and you don't bring them out of the rain/provide shelter from the sun you are failing to provide suitable shelter and breaking the law. One of the main problems with restricting the movement of your goat is that they must be moved every few hours. It is also now considered quite cruel by a lot of people, as goats are free roaming animals.

There are also some dangers involved in tying up your animal if they are going to have access to enrichments and play as they could become entangled and choke. Tethering isn't really a good long-term solution.

Tethering does have its advantages though. If you need to restrict access to grazing for health reasons, then tethering with a rope is a much simpler and more practical alternative to moving fencing or to having a dedicated restricted grazing area. It's also good for while you're fixing or replacing fencing, so that your goats can still go out to graze.

Fencing is massively important, though. Goats are notoriously difficult to confine, and they are hard on fencing—especially the cheaper kinds. One good choice for smaller areas is what's known as stock panels.

These are made of 1/4″ welded rod and come in 16-ft. lengths, 48 inches high. Other options are limited to such fencing as woven wire, chain link, and electric—either the common single-strand type (typically using 2-3 strands), the high-tensile variety, or the netting often referred to as "New Zealand" type fencing. Goats can be trained to respect electric fencing.

One acre of grazing will require 825 feet of fencing—and more if it's not square. Get prices on the kind of fencing you'd like and then add 10% per year for repairs.

Even the little Boer goats are good jumpers and can be very destructive. Just because they are smaller than other types of goat, doesn't mean they don't need such strong fencing and robust enclosures. One thing that Boer owners really enjoy about their goats is their stout nature and vigour.

2. Food and treats

Boers are fantastic animals, but because of their nature as meat animals they tend to overeat and get fat if allowed to eat what they want. Access to fresh grass and plants/ hay in winter is essential, but be careful of feeding supplements.

A basic diet of hay and clean drinking water should be supplemented by 2-8 oz of concentrates a day, depending on age and condition. This may not seem like much, as it is the same recommendation for Pygmy goats, but Boers will convert food into fat rather than milk, and can have real issues with obesity. Boer goats are browsers not grazers - they should not be considered as lawnmowers. Vegetables and fruit should be added to their diet. Twigs, leaves, bark and some 'weeds' are the natural food of the goat and will be welcomed as a great treat. Care must be taken not to allow access to poisonous plants. New foods should be introduced gradually. All food must be clean and untainted.

Goats are ruminants. The term refers to the rumen, the large first compartment of the four-part stomach in which cellulose, mostly from forage, is broken down by organisms living there. This is the basis of feeding goats.

The key to the long-term health of your goat is keeping their diet varied. A varied diet that regularly changes and has new things in will help prevent the gut from getting lazy. A lazy gut can get surprised by sudden, unexpected changes and causes a painful and potentially fatal bloat.

Forage is the mainstay of the goat diet. Forage is things like hay, pasture plants, and browse from trees and bushes. Goats have a reputation for eating everything but they will usually only eat things that are good for them. They may seem odd, as they eat sticks and bark and those tough, woody bits of plants that we wouldn't even attempt. Such coarse materials are indigestible to the goat, but the rumen microbes break them down. You are feeding the microbes, and the microbes feed the goat.

Roughage is essential for goat nutrition. Grains are secondary. For many people the best, easiest and cheapest way to feed goats is to provide good leafy grass or hay, plus 1-2 small cups a day of a commercial goat feed (grain ration).

Others prefer feeding their goats on pasture as much as possible. This can be quite simple, or it can become management-intensive, with controlled rotational grazing, pasture maintenance and renovation, expensive fencing and predator control, to name a few concerns. Too much lush pasture can do real damage to a little goat.

Goats also need hay and goat feed to top up their diet and to keep them fed through the winter. Good quality hay can be a real boon for your milk production too.

Most goat feed available is high in vitamin e and selenium; this helps to avoid various illnesses. They will also be designed for dairy animals, with good levels of everything needed to keep the milk production high and the quality good.

Does who are in milk will need grain. Males will just get fat on too much grain and are greedy little things, so be careful when feeding a mixed herd. Wethers are also prone to get fat if fed the same as their female companions.

Lots of goat owners grow their own brassicas to eat and end up sharing them with their goats. A brassicas is a leafy, above ground, non-salad vegetable such as cabbage, cauliflower, sprouts and broccoli. These are great for goats and they love to nibble any leaves that are not yet cooked. Goats are a great way to use up the surplus and recycle leafy vegetables. Don't give them any cooked leftovers though - they aren't suited to eating cooked food. If you have the time, and space, you could even grow some just for the goats.

Your goat will also need access to salt licks to add minerals to their diet. In the wild, goats will find natural mineral deposits to lick to supplement their intake, but in captivity they need you to provide these things. You can use salt licks in a lot of the feeding toys and lickit toys.

Goats, like all animals, can be fussy about treats, but finding out what treats your goat likes and letting them have a little bit of a treat regularly can be very useful.

If you ever need to give your goat any medicine, and they aren't suspicious of treat time, then your life will be a lot easier, as you can disguise pills or liquid medicines in their favourite nibbles. Knowing what treats to use as a bribe also makes training much easier.

Peanuts

Some goats love peanuts, but they might prefer salted, unsalted or still in the shell. If you are giving them salted peanuts, you should restrict access to any salt licks or other dietary salt. Peanuts in their shells also add some good roughage to their diet.

Calf manna

Calf manna is a commercially available treat made from anise, high quality protein, linseed oil, yeast and carbs and is a great source of protein, carbohydrates and vitamins and minerals. Most goats really enjoy calf manna and will gobble it down, eating from your hand if they can. Don't give more than a couple of handfuls a week though – chubby goats aren't healthy goats! This is also good for any animals recovering from an illness where they have lost weight, such as anorexia, diarrhoea or other digestive problems. It can be used to bulk up animals that are struggling to put on or maintain weight, but if this is a problem that persists, contact your vet for advice.

Any weight problems can be symptomatic of something more sinister than just not being hungry yet.

Alfalfa

You can get alfalfa cubes for rabbits that goats really love too, but again, not too many. You can also grow alfalfa in a sprouter on your kitchen window from seed, or in window boxes outside. You can also scatter the seeds onto the ground where the pasture grows.

Christmas tree

Christmas trees are delicious. If you contact Christmas tree farms after Christmas, they usually will give you any that they've already cut down. Goats love Christmas trees. They are not only delicious; they make a great game and good scratching posts.

Chips and crisps

Unsalted chips, crisps and tortilla are also a favourite, as they are nice and crunchy, but don't give too many as they can have too much fat in them.

Apples

Chopped up apples are great too, but as they are quite sweet, not in massive amounts. A couple of slices each will be a great treat and won't make them ill. Crab apples are also enjoyed by goats and are smaller so that they can eat whole apples. A couple of crab apple trees in the pasture will be well received and kept under control by the goats.

Carrots

Carrots, on the other hand, aren't too sweet and goats still love them. Carrots have a good nutritional content and are a good, healthy treat.

A lot of goats are partial to a Boer cookie here and there, but these can be very sweet and should not be given too often.

Seeds

Sunflower seeds are a great source of oils and fatty acids and are usually appreciated by goats. They also love getting the pine seeds out of pinecones and the pinecone can be a game in itself!

Breakfast cereals

Breakfast cereals make great treats. Frosted ones have too much sugar for a large regular snack, but as an occasional bribe they're ok.

A good guide for what your goats can browse on is grass and any of these plants:

- Acorns are ok for goats, but they can only have a little, as the hard shells can irritate the stomach and gut.
- Agapanthas is a good weed for goats, but they can only eat the leaves. The tubers and roots can be toxic to goats, although goats won't really eat the roots unless they are starving.
- Althea
- Angel Wing Bigoneas
- Apple leaves and bark will also be gobbled up greedily, so be careful, as goats will easily kill young apple trees by stripping them.
- Bamboo will be eaten happily by goats, but you should be careful to only let them have soft young shoots and leaves, as the older shoots can be too hard and can splinter and irritate or damage the digestive system.
- Banana, entire plant, fruit & peel.
- Bay Tree Leaves, both green and dried, are delicious and goats will eat these happily.

- Beans are good for goats. You can sew them into the ground as the plants are nitrogen fixers and improve soil quality at the same time as feeding goats. Boers will gratefully eat the whole plant, pods, leaves and stem.
- Beets, leaves and root, are good for goats, especially if they are producing milk. They have a high concentration of calcium and iron.
- Blackberry bushes, leaves, stem and all, are eaten by goats and goats can really help to keep them under control.
- Black Locus will be eaten whole by goats; they will eat and destroy the whole plants.
- Broccoli has a high concentration of calcium, vitamins and iron are good for goats, especially if they are producing milk. You can sew the seeds into the ground or your pasture and just let the shoots grow themselves.
- Cabbage is much the same as broccoli, in that it is an excellent source of calcium, vitamins and iron, and they can also be sewn into the pasture.
- Camellias will be pruned away by goats.
- Collard Greens are like broccoli and cabbage in their nutritional content and growing.
- Carrots are usually really loved by goats, although there are a few that won't even eat them. Carrots are very sweet, so too much might make them fat. They can eat the whole carrot plant, tops and all.
- Catnip can be eaten by goats, but many won't.
- Both clover and comfrey are good for goats and can be sewn into the ground to improve soil quality and both will be gobbled up by goats.
- Cottonwood
- Coyote Bush
- Dandelion is a fantastic source of vitamins and minerals. The leaves and the roots must be delicious to goats, as they will hunt them out first from the pastures.
- Douglas Fir
- Dogwood
- Elm

- Fava Bean pods
- Fern is another delicacy that goats prize and will eat first.
- Fescue grass
- Ficus
- Grape, entire plants
- Greenbrier
- Hemlock Trees are very different to the poisonous hemlock, and goats can happily eat the leaves of the hemlock tree, which are sweet and tasty.
- Hibiscus is high in carotene, vitamins and minerals and the metal trace amounts are good for warding off many illnesses.
- Honeysuckle will be eaten whole and greedily by goats. They really love the sweet leaves and flowers.
- The traditional gout cure, hyssop, is great for goats, as it is a fantastic digestive aid, and reduces the likelihood of bloat.
- Ivy is fine for goats, true ivy, mind; poison ivy will cause your goat all sorts of digestive discomfort, and can cause bloat and irritate the gut.
- Jackfruit leaves
- Jade
- Jambolan leaves
- Japanese Elm
- Japanese Knotweed aka: polygonum cuspidatum aka: fallopia japonica. This is a real boon if you find you do have Knotweed on your land, as goats will really go for it and clip it down before it gets strong enough to spread.
- Japanese Magnolias (blooms/leaves)
- Johoba
- Kudzu
- Lilac bark /branches
- Lupine – the seeds are the part of the plant that are the greatest problem.
- Magnolia Leaves green and dried
- Mango leaves
- Manzanita (Arctostaphylos)

- Maple Trees, leaves & bark - (goats will readily strip the bark and kill the tree) you need to make sure that you are not feeding RED maple as it CAN KILL goats.
- Marijuana-in moderation
- Mesquite
- Mint
- Mock Orange
- Monkey-flower
- Mountain Ash trees make an excellent foraging exercise for goats, as they strip the bark and snaffle up the leaves.
- Morning Glory
- Moss
- Mulberry
- Mullein
- Mustard
- Nettles will be happily eaten by Boer goats, and they crop them quite low which is nice, as you can wear shorts in the enclosure without fear of being stung!
- Lemon Grass
- Oak Tree Leaves
- Patterson's Curse
- Pea plants, like beans, are good for goats and you can sew them into the ground as the plants are nitrogen fixers and improve soil quality at the same time as feeding goats. Boers will gratefully eat the whole plant, pods, leaves and stem.
- Peanuts, including the shells
- Pear bark and leaves will be snaffled up greedily by goats, as will the fruit.
- Pencil cacti are delicate, slender plants that grow happily in the southern United States. A lot of goat owners have pencil cactus in the pasture, and they are quite edible.
- Peppers and pepper plants will be devoured whole by a hungry Boer, they love them!
- Pine Trees are an absolute favourite of most goats, but they will happily eat the whole thing and can kill off entire hedgerows if they can reach right to the top of all of the plants.

- Plum trees are another plant that can find themselves in trouble if your goat can get at them. You need to make sure that they don't eat the stones of the fruit, though, as these can be poisonous.
- Privet
- Pumpkin is delicious and if you manage to get any started you can pop some of the plants in with the goats. My neighbour grows pumpkins for shows and will often start a few hundred plants off, and give the weaker plants to the goats, usually only ending up with a dozen or so plants at the end. Goats like the leaves, stems, flowers and fruit of pumpkins, so this is a win-win plant (unless you were hoping to keep some for yourself!)
- Pomegranates
- Poplar Trees
- Raspberry, entire plant (goats loves raspberry)
- Red-tips
- Rose, all, entire plant (goats loves roses)
- Rhubarb Leaves
- Salvation Jane
- Sassafras
- Silver Berry
- Southern Bayberry (myrica cerifera)
- Spruce trees
- Sumac, the tree
- Sunflowers
- Strawberry plants are delicious for goats. They are a good source of vitamin C and carbohydrates.
- Sweet Gum Trees
- Sweet potato leaves
- Tomatoes (cherry tomatoes make wonderful treats)
- Tomato plants- in moderation (mine eat them with no problems)
- Tree of Heaven
- Turnips
- Yaupon Holly (Ilex vomitoria)
- Yarrow
- Yellow Locus
- Yucca

- Vetch
- Virginia Creeper
- Wandering Jew
- Watermelon
- Wax Myrtle is a really good treat for goats, there
- Weeping Willow
- Wild Rose. Goats will snaffle up the entire plant! They love the flowers too.
- Wild Tobacco

All of these plats are appreciated by goats, but they can kill trees that they like, so make sure that they don't have access to any trees that you are fond of!

You need to make sure your goats have access to a constant supply of fresh, clean water.

There are many plants that are POISONOUS to goats. While Boers are big, sturdy animals, with a relatively high tolerance of poisonous plant, you do still need to keep a specific eye out for the following plants:
- African Rue
- Andromeda (related to foxglove)
- Avocado- South American Avocado leaves/tree such as Haas or crosses with Haas
- Avocado- Fuarte (definitely)
- Azalea
- Brouwer's Beauty Andromeda
- Boxwood
- Burning Bush berries
- Calotropis
- Cassava (manioc)
- China Berry Trees, all parts
- Choke Cherries, wilting especially
- Choke Cherry Leaves in abundance
- Datura
- Dog Hobble

- Dumb Cane (diffenbachia) (Houseplant)
- Euonymus Bush berries
- False Tansy
- Foxglove
- "Fiddleneck"- know by this common name in CA. It is a fuzzy looking, 12" to 15" plant, with small, yellow blossoms, - stem shaped like the neck of a fiddle.
- Flixweed
- Fusha
- Holly Trees/Bushes
- Ilysanthes floribunda
- Japanese pieris (extremely toxic)
- Japanese Yew
- Lantana
- Larkspur- a ferny, flowering plant in shades of blue, pink and white.
- Lasiandra
- Lilacs
- Lily of the Valley (Pieris Japonica)
- Lupine - appears on both lists: the seeds are the part of the plant that are the greatest problem.
- Madreselva (Spain) patologia renal
- Maya-Maya
- Monkhood
- Milkweed
- Mountain Laurel
- Nightshade – some people allow their goats nightshade and it does them no harm, but it has been known to kill goats, even the big-boned Boer.
- Oleander
- Pieris Japonica (extremely toxic)
- Red Maples kill goats of all sizes, and is best avoided all together to keep goats safe.
- Rhododendron are not only highly invasive, but the waxy leaves can be very poisonous.
- Rhubarb leaves
- Tu Tu (the Maori name for Coriaria arborea)

45

- Wild Cherry, the wilted leaves are fine. They are highly poisonous but fresh and dried leaves can be safe. A lot of goat owners don't risk it, as the wilted leaves contain prussic acid that degrades to cyanide.
- Yew

Chapter 5) Settling in your goat

Before getting your goat, if you live in the UK you need a CPH
number (county parish holding number). This is very easy to
obtain, but it is illegal to own any livestock without one. Some
houses have a covenant on them that bar you from keeping any
livestock, though there are very few such covenants.
In the USA, you need to check if you can keep one in your city.
(you can find out on http://www.municode.com/) In most parts of
the country you can keep them with the correct permits, but this is
different for all 50 states.
In Australia, you need a registered brand, a PIC (property
identification code) and a registered earmark. (you can find out
more at www.agric.wa.gov.au) If you don't comply you can be
fined $5,000.

Goats are incredibly intelligent and have a great deal of emotional
reactions and responses to things you'd never imagine. So it is
important that you take the time to think about your goats'
emotional needs as well as their physical needs before moving
them in with you. You will be completely responsible for your
goat's physical and emotional wellbeing.
Just like if you were bringing home a new puppy or a baby, you
will need to have everything ready for the new addition to your
household.

As they are herd animals, you need to consider the emotional
wellbeing of your goat when they come to you. Getting a lot of
goats on your first venture into goat ownership is not a good idea.
So what do you do? It's probably a good idea to get a doe with a
kid at foot, so she won't be lonely.
If you already have goats, sheep or even horses or alpacas then
you're sorted. Mixed species herds are fairly common among
small holders and can be seen in the wild. For evidence of this,

you can turn to youtube. There are lots of videos of goats gambolling about with horses, sheep and even dogs.

As long as you are not bringing your goat home on their own, then you don't need to worry about your new additions. A good way to make sure your goats don't come home lonely is to bring them home with a couple of young wethers.

1. Bonding

You need spend a lot of time bonding with your goat. Goats, like children and dogs, respond to tones of voice. Always use a soft, soothing tone when you are near your goat. It will relax him/her. You should spend time around your goat when you are calm and relaxed to make sure that your goat recognises you as being safe. Your goat needs to be able to trust you; you'll be milking it, and that requires trust on both parts. You should make sure your goat knows that you will never let them down. If he has an itch, scratch it for him. Never do big, sudden movements that could spook them.

You should groom your goat as much as possible, stroking them, being around them, and getting them used to the idea that you are a source of possible comfort. Express your feelings for your goat in a way that he/she always will understand and don't be ambiguous.

Don't pull away if the goat tries to sniff or nibble on you. He/she is simply returning your affection, and will be confused if you don't accept it. Watch the way goats interact with each other. They nibble each other when they are happy and content. Hold your hand out and let it smell you; if you let your goat get used to your scent, it will also help you to bond.

2. Preparing for your goat

There are lots of things you need to do to make your goat feel at home. Bring them home, give them access to food and water and let them acclimatise to their surroundings before trying to interact with them.

If your goat is in milk, make sure you know their routine and milk them when their schedule demands. Then you can adjust their timetable gently to suit yours. You should also know how to milk the goat before she arrives. – your breeder should be able to show you this in person, and you can read chapter 6 to give you a good idea about milking.

It is also a good idea to find out what your goat ate before they came to you and feed them this as they adjust, as sudden changes in diet can make goats quite ill.

You should have the housing and pasture prepared before they move in. You should try to remove as much of any plants from the poisons list as you can. If you have the time and can borrow the equipment it is a good idea to turn in the seeds of some of the plants from the list in chapter 4.

3. Shopping list

There are a few things you should have before your goat comes home, both for their long-term comfort and just in case anything happens:
- Ivermectin
- Grass keep
- Feed
- Hay
- Milking stool and pale
- Antiseptic

- Wormer
- Toys
- Styptic
- Vaccines
- Loperamide (diarrhoea medication such as Imodium)
- Electrolyte compound
- Table salt

By having these items just in case, you won't find yourself hunting for an all night supermarket that stocks Imodium so that your kids don't die from diarrhoea related dehydration while you're trying to get hold of a vet who can come out, or suddenly realise that it's milking time and you have none of the equipment yet.

4. Logbook

As an animal owner and enthusiast for all things ordered, I go on and on about logbooks. A logbook or some sort of general record may well save your goat's life one day. It can make everything easier in the long run too.

For many goat owners a logbook may be a little OTT in the way of being organised, but it can literally be a lifesaver. By keeping precise records that can be accessed and understood by anyone who might need to require information about your goat's habits, behaviour, feeding and medications, you will be keeping your goat safe, even if you are not the only one to be looking after them. It could even mean you might be able to go on holiday one day, though that's doubtful, as livestock takes over your life. It can mean your vet may be able to pinpoint the sources or beginning of any illnesses. This will also be useful if you come to sell your goat later on.

The back pages should be a calendar, with dates not days, where you can mark on the worming, farrier and vaccine dates. If you do these things to a strict routine, then there will be far less problems of overlap or missing them out. This is also very useful if there are two or more people involved in the care of the animal.

Keeping a record of any medical intervention is very handy too, and knowing when exactly they are administered can help to identify bad interactions.

The front pages should contain a list of useful phone numbers (vet, farrier, insurance details), any regular medications the animal is taking and their description/passport information. This can be very useful in case there are any problems when someone else is watching your goat, for example when you are on holiday. Internal pages should be a week or 2 per page with a line about each visit to the goat. You should record feed given, any changes in the movement/gait of the goat, interactions with other animals etc. You should also make a record of any time your goat is in transit and how they react to this. If they are ever weighed or measured, you should write this down. If they don't seem to have been eating or drinking this should also be noted.

By keeping good records of feed, behaviour, habits, routine and medications, your goats will be safe, whoever has to look after them.

Chapter 6) Milking your goat

Not all goats need milking. If you want Boers as just pets, you can get a couple of wethers – castrated males – or don't breed from your females. This will mean that you have goats just as companion animals, and they can be a lot of fun to have gambolling about in your field. An increasing number of people keep Boers simply as pets, not to be milked at all.

Even though Boers are big girls, you will probably need a milking stand for them as it stops them from wandering off as easily and it protects you from a seriously bad back. A good milking stand and a stool can make milking much more comfortable for both you and your goat.

When a doe freshens (comes into milk at kidding), she doesn't produce as much milk as she will later because her kids don't need that much yet. Production increases for two months or so and slowly declines. This lactation curve matches kid growth and decreasing reliance on milk. Kids are nutritionally self-sufficient at about 10 weeks old. In other words, most does produce milk at the rate the kids need it. Lactation persistence means that a good milker's production stays at its peak for a long time.

Milking takes dedication, time and patience. You need to be able to remain calm in the face of disappointment. It is very important to milk twice daily at 12-hour intervals to maintain production. Some people milk at 6, 2 and 10, but this isn't really necessary. Milking twice is absolutely vital though. When milk is in the udder for 18 hours, the milk producing cells (alveoli) begin to shut down due to pressure. Once this production is lost, it cannot be regained. As we all know, goats definitely like their routine, so regular milking times keep them happy and comfortable.
The best way to start is to start milking your goats just after the kids are born. You milk her just after kidding, so she accepts you

as her kid. That will mean you will have to bottle feed the babies sometimes, to make sure they have enough milk, but that creates a special bond, as you join in with their natural mother, both feeding the babies and milking the mother. Some people suggest taking the kids away all together, but this isn't for everyone, and you can milk mum and leave the kids at foot.

Does with mastitis are always milked last to prevent spreading bacteria to the next udder. Sanitation management is very important in avoiding mastitis. Milk from does with mastitis isn't fit for consumption, but continue cleaning and milking until it clears up or she will dry off.

This is going to be said over and over again – keeping everything clean is absolutely vital. Wash everything thoroughly before and after each use. If you can't remember whether or not you've done it, wash it again.

Wash and dry your hands before you are going to milk. It is unnecessary to wash the entire udder before milking, but washing and drying each teat helps prevent mastitis. Wash each teat with a separate towel and discard. Dry each teat with a separate paper towel and discard. Never reuse a towel. (Teats can also be sanitized by pre-dipping and drying each one with a separate paper towel instead of washing.)

Boer does can be very active and have a great time running about, but you need them to calm down before milking. Make sure that, if your doe is on the excitable side, she is calm before you milk her, as she needs to be calm in order to produce oxytocin. Letting milk down is a response to oxytocin, and without it milking will be difficult, if not imporssible. Oxytocin is the same chemical that helps mothers and babies bond and it is vital that a doe is relaxed. When a doe is excited or upset, she releases adrenaline, which cancels oxytocin, and it is impossible for her to give milk until the adrenaline is used up. When it is, it takes another few minutes of preparation to elicit another oxytocin response. Loud, unusual noise or movements stir up a fear response, causing the release of adrenaline, so a calm routine is always required. You can massage the shoulders, neck and face of your Boer to calm her down.

Udder preparation relaxes the doe so she will let her milk down. Massage the udder for 30 seconds or so after washing to feel udder texture. Lumps, hot spots or injuries may be found at this time.

Examine the first few streams of milk from each teat for abnormalities and discard the initial streams, as they are more likely to be contaminated than later milk.
The dark, perforated insert in a strip cup lets milk though while retaining clots or strings so that you can check for anything out of the ordinary. The Boer doe usually gives a little stream of milk, and a clean, dark cloth or a dark-coloured dish works well. Check the milk from each teat at each milking. The first few streams of milk contain the most bacteria, so it is a good idea to discard this anyway.

Try to completely empty the udder within five minutes after udder preparation - oxytocin response is the greatest during those five minutes. Grasp the base of each teat just below the udder floor with your thumb, index and middle fingers.

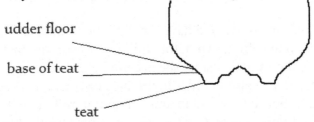

udder floor

base of teat

teat

Delicate tissue may be injured if you squeeze any part of the udder. Milk in the teat cistern is trapped when you squeeze the base of the teat with your thumb and index finger. Expel the milk using all 4 fingers in a rolling motion, your middle finger following the index finger in gentle squeezing. Pulling on the teat or sliding your fingers down it may injure udder or teat tissue. Alternate the streams, left and right.

Developing coordination takes time - don't give up – you can practice on a rubber glove with a pinprick in it if you are nervous of hurting her. Ask the breeder when you collect her to demonstrate and if they can show you how. These people love their goats and are usually more than happy to help you learn how to milk properly and will be pleased if you defer to their experience and knowledge.

Your hands may tire and cramp, but it gets easier as you build up milking muscles and coordination. At the end of the milking, massage the udder to release the last of the milk and milk that out. This is called stripping. It is important to strip out each time you milk to make sure no milk stands in the udders for any length of time and to keep the udders healthy.

After milking, dip the entire length of each teat with a good teat dip to kill bacteria at the orifice and help close the orifices. Teat dipping is very important.

If you have to reconstitute a dip, it is important to make it the proper strength. Strong solutions can damage the skin, and it is ineffective if it is too weak. Follow the label directions. Ideally, fresh teat dip is used on each teat at each milking. Contaminated teat dip is no longer effective and may harbour bacteria. I use a small glass jar with a 1"-deep plastic lid. I snap off the lid, fill it about 3/4 full, coat each teat, and discard the used portion. Besides the quality of the dip, good coverage is the most important part of dipping. A drop of teat dip should be visible on the end of each teat. (Fight-Bac teat spray also works very well instead of dipping.) After dipping or spraying, keep the doe standing for 15 minutes or so, maybe with fresh hay in the manger. If she lies down, the udder can be re-contaminated and the teat dip won't work as well as it should.

Milk is a delicate product and should be filtered immediately after milking to remove hair and other contaminants. Then it should be cooled as quickly as possible. Milk filters are available at feed stores and catalogue suppliers. Strain into a glass jar and refrigerate immediately.

Milking sounds complex, but it is very easy. Having the right equipment is a big help. Good habits in procedure and technique are important in the long run, both for your enjoyment of the milking process and maintaining the health of your does.

Having the right tools of the trade make milking more pleasurable and preserve milk quality and udder health. Milking equipment must be kept very clean between uses, and it is best to let it air dry after it is washed. You'll need a few things, other than a goat, in order to milk your goat.
- A stand
- Food or treats to keep them occupied if they fret
- A stool
- A pale
- Some udder washing solution

Boer goats produce very creamy milk with very high buttermilk content and lots of protein, making it great for all sorts of added value dairy products, likes cheese, butter and yoghurt. Because of this most Boer owners choose their goats as dairy animals. If your goat is for milking, you need to know how to milk the animal and be able to milk them regularly. They need milking every 12 hours and it is cruel to milk them less often than this, as it can be very uncomfortable.
Some people think that they don't like the taste of goats' milk and that it has a "goaty" taste. This is only ever because of bacteria fouling the milk, which can almost always be avoided by cleaning your hands and the udder thoroughly. The whole milking area should be scrupulously clean and free from any potential contaminants. There should be no males allowed near the milking area, as they smell and the milk will absorb the smell.
A lot of goat owners do their milking in a separate space where the goats would not be at all in their normal daily routine. This is not only great for keeping the milk free from contaminants by goaty hair and smells, but it's good for training your goat. If she knows that when she goes to a certain place she is going to be milked, she will learn that when she is there she should prepare to

be milked, by getting on the stand or positioning herself to be milked.

Lots of goats that know their milking routine will wait by the gate to the milking area when their udders are feeling uncomfortable. This has many advantages and lets owners know when the animal needs to be milked. This improves the relationship between the owner and the goat as well as the quality and quantity of milk produced, especially if it increases the regularity at which you milk your goat, i.e. you milk on request.

Once you're in the swing of it, milking gets easy and becomes a simple part of your daily routine with your animal. It should eventually be a calming time when you both feel safe and close. First of all, warm up your hands. Rub them together or stick them down your jumper or something. No one likes a cold shock. Then, take the teat in your hand. Close off the top of the teat with your thumb and forefinger so the milk in the teat will be forced out of the teat, not back into the udder.

Next close your second finger, then the third, and finally your pinkie, forcing the milk out of the teat. Use steady pressure in a rolling motion without pinching or squeezing the teat at all. You can practice this action by placing your fingers on the palm of your hand and pushing down gently with each finger in turn. This way you can feel that you are making an even, rolling pressure. Discard the first stream from each teat, as it will be high in bacteria, will taste goaty and can foul up the whole batch. This is often the cause of the unpleasant taste people associate with goat's milk. If you always remember to keep this out of the milk you keep then you end up with a much nicer end product for yourself.

Once you've got rid of the first stream, you can start the milking process properly; remember that rolling motion with your fingers to avoid pulling or rubbing the teats. Repeat this process with your other hand on the other teat. Alternate like this until the milk flow ceases. You do need to make sure you completely strip out (empty) the udders to encourage milk production to stay high.

Milk should be weighed and recorded. Weight is used rather than volume because the numbers are easier to work with but also to eliminate guesswork caused by foam.

Strain the warm milk using an approved filter, and cool it immediately and thoroughly. Milk should be chilled to 38° within one hour. The best way to achieve this is by placing the milk container in a pan of ice water for 15-20 minutes, stirring occasionally. Then it can be refrigerated.

Goat massage

While this isn't technically necessary for milking your goat, it is a useful skill to have to calm them down and is handy for keeping milking a positive, calming experience. Goats are much more productive when they are calm.

Face and head massage is a good way to start getting your goat calm. A light massage on the head with the fingertips is a nice way to stimulate the brain, blood circulation and natural oils in the skin and will aid relaxation. Place both hands either side of the head under the ears and push your fingertips into the fur. Using small, regular circle motions towards the back of the head, up, forwards and down again, gentle begin to massage the goat's head and face. You should do this symmetrically. Move your hands to the top of the head and do the same circular movements. Then you can stroke along the nose with both hands, your index fingers pulling forwards and down, in front of the eyes and past the cheekbones. Rub the rears, gently stroking with the direction of the fur with your thumbs on the underside or skin side and your fingers on the outside.

A back massage on goats is often very similar to stroking. Lightly rest the flat palm of your hand on top of your goat's head or neck. Make long, sweeping passes along the length of the spine and down the tail. Repeat this several times slowly. You can gradually increase your pressure if your goat likes it. Do not press straight down on the lower part of the back. To finish, allow one hand to rest at the base of your goat's head and the other hand to rest over the area of the pelvis (the high point over your goat's hips). These two areas correspond to the part of the spinal cord that controls the rest and relaxation responses of the body. Then massage with small circles with your thumbs on either side of the spine. You can also use your fingers to "walk" along the spine. This feels great and helps with overall circulation, lymphatic drainage and spinal health. Next, use a very light kneading motion over tight muscles (like kneading dough), to help loosen the muscle fibbers and stimulate deeper circulation. Make sure to massage the neck and shoulders because your goat will most likely adore you for it!

A goat, like us, can carry a lot of tension in its legs. If your goat is comfortable with you, you can massage the legs too. This isn't usually done on younger goats, but as they get older they can tend to seize up, just like us. Removing this tension can lead to a higher milk yield for longer.

Take one of the legs up and hold the hoof in one hand. With the other hand, apply gentle pressure all along the leg from top to bottom. Then do the same thing in the other direction – from the hoof to the shoulder/hip. Repeat 3-4 times with each leg. Use the gentle kneading motion around the hips and buttocks. Remember, do not work directly over arthritic or painful/inflamed joints; work on the muscles around them. Do some easy stretching exercises to help the joints and surrounding tissues with mobility and flexibility. Gently bend and flex arthritic joints to improve range of motion. Goat's legs are very fragile, and if they begin to squirm, let them go to avoid damage.

Tummy rubs are nice, aren't they? During pregnancy and in general a tummy rub is very relaxing for both goats and humans. Place your hands either side of her tummy and rub in circles, gently. Move the circles forwards and backwards and down underneath the tummy. This is very relaxing and is a great way to bond with your goat.

Chapter 7) Using goats' milk

It's odd to think, but the meat bred Boer has exceptionally high milk solids of very good quality. This makes it perfect for cheese, kefir, yoghurt etc, you name a value added milk product, Boer milk is good for it.

Surprising as it might seem, more people consume goat's milk than they do cow's milk. As unbelievable as this may sound, it is true. Most third world countries and quite a few European countries prize goats and goat's milk over cow's milk. There are so many useful things you can do with goat's milk, and as your goat could produce as much as 2-3 litres a day you might need to find an alternative use for the milk.

The people who know and love you will all be aware you have a goat, and may well be a little jealous, and why wouldn't they be? So making things from your milk to give to people is not only a cheep alternative to Christmas presents, but will also be a thoughtful and meaningful gift.

As a lot of people who are lactose intolerant can have goat's milk products, you can imagine how much joy you could give to lactose intolerant friends and family members with delicious produce that they can actually enjoy without the worry of health repercussions.

There are also lots of studies currently being done on the health benefits of raw milk. There's lots of anecdotal evidence that raw milk reduces instances of allergies and asthma, but the research is still in its infancy at the moment.

In a lot of the developed world it is difficult to sell and get hold of raw milk. In the UK, farmers can sell it directly from the farm. In a lot of the United States it is illegal to transport raw milk across state lines. In Australia and New Zealand the movement of raw milk is strictly controlled. Because of this, the easiest way to get hold of raw milk is often to produce it yourself.

You can do all sorts of things with goats' milk. Goats' milk cheese is delicious and healthier than cow's milk cheese. The butter is also very tasty and making it can really help you keep fit/burn off the excess calories you take in from the butter itself. If all that bashing about isn't to your taste, then goats' milk yoghurt is great pouring yoghurt for breakfast and adding to smoothies. Oh and the ice cream! As an ice cream enthusiast it is difficult to contain yourself when talking about goats' milk ice cream. There are a lot of other foods that goats' milk is a great base for, including some rather good soups. You can also make a great, hearty bread using goat's milk. There is also a tasty drink called Kefir that is strange yet delicious and can be made form goat's milk.

Last but not least, the soaps and lotions that you can make from goat's milk is said to have all sorts of healthy properties for your skin, as well as making a fabulous gift. Goat's milk is high in vitamins and minerals, particularly vitamin A, which aids in repairing damaged skin. It is also naturally rich in caprylic acid, which soothes and rejuvenates skin.

Goat's milk has fantastic moisturising properties and contains something called alpha hydroxy acid, which a lot of cosmetic companies say reduces the appearance of wrinkles, removes dead skin cells and is generally tip top for your skin. And if you have goats, you don't have to pay anyone extortionate amounts of money for something that may or may not work.

Kefir

Most people have never heard of kefir (pronounced kefear, not key fur as I was saying when I asked about it). Kefir is like a thin drinking yoghurt. There are reams of medical studies with positive results using kefir. They have been conducted for conditions that include diabetes, high cholesterol levels, high blood pressure and many more. It is also a good pro-biotic and is good for recovering from or preventing any gut problems.

If you like kefir, you can use the grains to make it from other things like different types of milk, sugar water, soya or rice milk or even fruit juice.

It is very simple to make and doesn't take very long at all. You just need milk and kefir grains. They look like squishy little cauliflowers and you can buy them online.

Just place the milk kefir grains in milk, give it a quick stir with a non-metal spoon, cover loosely (a towel works great), and allow the kefir to culture on the side for 12 to 24 hours.

After 12 hours, check the kefir every few hours (if possible) so you can remove the kefir grains once the mixture reaches the desired consistency. If your home is on the cool side, it can take a few hours longer for the milk kefir to culture.

Keep the grains as instructed on the packaging and you'll never need to buy any more ever again!

Cheese

There are a number of cheeses you can make with goats milk, from lovely, creamy, soft cheeses like Chevre to sliceable, hard cheeses that can be cut into chunks and served on sticks, if that is the sort of thing you do.

Whatever sort of cheese you're making, they all start off the same way – with milk.

You don't need to pasteurise the milk, but some bacteria can really mess up your cheese and make it at best unpalatable. So you need to heat-treat the milk to stop the germs fouling up your cheese.

Heat the milk on the stove, stirring to stop it burning and when it reaches 65C, hold it there for a few minutes. Then allow it to cool to room temperature.

Then just add a cheese culture. You can buy a cheese culture online for very little, and they usually come freeze fried. Follow the instructions on the package and stir up thoroughly. Then leave it for half an hour or so.

Then you add rennet to the mix and stir from the bottom up, for about a minute, before leaving to settle for 12-24 hours. By this time there will be a thin layer of whey on top of the curd that you can pour off.

From this basic beginning you can make all sorts of cheeses.

For soft cheese (Boursin type), tie the curd in a cheesecloth and hang for a day to drain. Then salt to taste and add herbs, pepper and garlic.

For Chevre type cheese, drain the curds in a mould with holes poked in. Plastic cups are good for this, as you can poke holes in them quite easily. After 2 days, take it out of the mould and salt the sides.

Line a cheese mould (or a can of some sort with holes in it) with cheesecloth and scoop the curds into it. Once the curds have settled (half an hour or so) add more curds to the top.

Then you need to put in something called a follower. This is something smaller than the mould that you can put the weights on as you weigh down the cheese as it develops. After 2 days you can remove the cheese from the mould and store in the fridge until it's ready.

If you want to make an aged cheese, or give it as a gift, you can dip the hard cheese in cheese wax and it will be storable for up to 6 months.

For other types of cheese, or more detailed instructions, there are some fantastic books and websites. A quick Internet search will come up with loads of great recipes. You can make Feta types, fruity types and cream cheese types.

Yoghurt

Goat's milk yoghurt is a lot thinner than cow's milk yoghurt, and is like most Greek yoghurt – that's what Greek yoghurt is!

Use a litre and a half of milk and 60mls of live yoghurt – preferably goat's milk yoghurt.

In a sturdy saucepan, bring your milk to a gentle boil over a medium heat, stirring often, and then simmer, stirring constantly, for 2 minutes. Pour into large glass bowl and let cool until you can hold your finger in the milk for 10 seconds. This will be after about 15 minutes of cooling; don't stick your finger in boiling milk- it will burn you.

In smaller bowl, whisk together yogurt and 2 tbsp (30 mL) of the warm milk until it's blended together nicely. Then stir that into the remaining warm milk. Cover with plastic wrap, then a tea towel and let it stand in draft-free place until thickened, about 12 hours. Cover and refrigerate until cold.
You can keep this in the fridge for up to a week and it goes nicely with fruit, cereal and ice cream.

Ice cream
Because goat's milk generally has less water, more fat, less lactose and more solids than cow's milk, it makes a thick, creamy, delicious ice cream with a very good flavour. Boer milk is especially good for ice cream as it has good fat content.
A basic vanilla ice cream can be made like this:
- 2 cups goat milk
- -½ vanilla bean or 1 tablespoon of vanilla extract
- 4 egg yolks
- ⅓ cup honey
- 1 tablespoon of corn starch

Mix together the egg yolks, ½ cup of goat's milk and the cornstarch until smooth in a blender.
If using a vanilla bean, split it and scrape out the seeds. Add the pod and seeds to the goat's milk in the next step. If using vanilla extract, it will be added in at the end of the cooking process.
Add the remaining goat's milk and honey to a heavy bottomed, medium saucepan (preferably one with a pouring lip), and bring to a rolling boil on a medium heat. Boil, stirring for 3 minutes. Remove the saucepan from the burner. Turn the blender on at a low setting and in a very, very thin stream pour in the hot goat's milk. It is critical that this is done very slowly so as not to end up with scrambled eggs. Do this through the access hole in your blender lid as opposed to just having the lid off; otherwise you risk making a surprising and regrettable mess.

When the goat's milk mix is fully incorporated with the eggs, turn off the blender and pour the mix back into the pan you used to heat the goat's milk.

Thicken the mixture into an egg custard by stirring constantly, over a medium heat, until you measure 170° F/77° C on a good instant read thermometer. If you don't have an instant read thermometer, thicken it until you can run your finger over the back of the spoon or spatula you are stirring with and leave a trail that doesn't immediately fill back in.

Remove from the heat. Remove the two pieces of vanilla bean pod. If using vanilla extract instead, mix it in now.

Pre-chill the mixture before freezing it in your ice cream maker.

Freeze the mixture in your ice cream maker. It should take 15 – 30 minutes.

Serve right out of your maker or later from your freezer. Store the remainder in a freezer proof container. A layer of cling wrap smoothed on to the top of the ice cream before you close the container will help keep air out and frost from forming.

You can add other flavours to this and leave out the vanilla. For example, ginger syrup and crystallised ginger make a great, zingy ice cream that really impresses.

Or you can do a chocolate chunk ice cream with cocoa and sugar in the mix and throwing in some high quality chocolate pieces at the end.

Or in the summer you can add fresh hedgerow fruit, like raspberries or blackberries, to make a refreshing ripple of flavour.

Bread

Bread made with goat's milk is a delicious, hearty addition to the table. The fat in the milk makes for a great texture in the bread, and it keeps for up to 3 days as long as you don't put it in the fridge - the cold, dry air in the fridge crystallises the bread, making it go stale quicker.

You need:
- 250g strong white bread flour

- 1 tsp fast-action dried yeast
- 1 tbsp olive oil
- 200ml goat's milk
- Salt

Mix together the flour, yeast and 1/2 tsp salt. Add the oil, then pour in the water gradually, adding enough to make a soft dough. Knead the dough on a lightly floured surface for about 4-5 mins until the dough feels strong and stretchy. The key to good bread is elasticity.

Put on a floured baking tray in a warm place while the dough rises or proves. Once it's doubled in size, knock the air out to redistribute the bubbles, give it a **quick** need and leave to rise again. Then bake the bread in a preheated oven at 210C for 45 mins or until the crust is crunchy. Then serve warm with hot soup.

Soup

Most vegetable soups can be truly complimented with goat's milk. In the winter, a nice, filling squash or carrot soup that is thick and creamy can really warm up the day.

This recipe is for squash, but you can substitute carrots, parsnips or any other winter vegetable, or use a mixture depending on what you have in.

You will need:
- 1 large squash – diced or sliced
- 6 tsp olive oil
- 6 cloves of peeled and crushed garlic, or a good dollop of the stuff from a tube
- 1 medium onion – diced
- 1 tsp pepper
- 2 pints of goats milk
- Pinch of salt.

Roast the squash (or whatever vegetable you're using) in a preheated oven at 170C for 30 minutes. Then add the garlic, olive oil and onion, mix everything up and return to the oven for another half an hour.

Put a quarter of the milk in a blender with the squash and everything else that's been roasted and whisk it up into a fine puree. Then put this in a pan and heat up. As it is heating, add more milk.

Do not allow to boil.

When the soup is hot enough, add the pepper to taste and serve with crusty bread and a dollop of butter.

Butter

Due to the high fat content of Boer milk, it is excellent for making butter. There is also high protein in Boer milk, which makes it a lot easier to use for butter. You need a pint of goat's cream to make butter. This means that you need to separate the cream from a few days worth of milking. To do this, you have to make sure that the milk sits undisturbed in the fridge for a day, then take the cream off, and use the rest of the milk in your tea or on your breakfast or whatever you normally do, and repeat this with another few days of milk.

Then you need to chill some beaters, water and a bowl in the fridge. These need to be properly cold by the time you use them. Then, heat up the cream using the temperature of the room until it's a little over 50F. The contrast in temperature here makes the process much easier.

Then whip up the cream until it's whipped like you'd put on a cake. Then keep going. Keep going until the cream begins to split. Keep going past the point where you'd have done it wrong if you were making whipped cream and then keep going some more.

Little globules of butter will be forming, surrounded by a thin, white liquid. As soon as the globules start to cluster together, stop whipping. You're done with that bit.

Next you just strain the butter, gently, in cheesecloth to let out the remaining liquid. You can use this in lotions or mix it in with pig feed.

Then turn the butter out into a dish or onto cling film and shape it and put it into the fridge.

Soap

If you're doing soap you need to be very careful of some of the chemicals used. GOGGLES AND GLOVES are an absolute must when you're dealing with lye, as you don't want your hands and eyes turning into soap. Seriously. Disgusting as it sounds, that can happen – just like human soap in bad gangster films – so be careful.

You will need:
- 26.5 oz. Olive oil
- 20 oz. frozen goats milk (freeze in ice cube tray)
- 16.5 oz Coconut oil
- 10 oz. Vegetable oil, preferably Rape Seed and not Palm Oil
- 209g Lye

You should use frozen goat's milk, as the Lye causes a chemical reaction with the liquid and gets very hot. Burning the milk messes everything up, so using it frozen really helps. You should also keep the mixture in a bowl that is inside another bowl of ice water.

Melt all the oils and fats together and leave to stand, but do not leave to set.

With your goggles and gloves on, pour the lye into the goat's milk ice/slush and stir constantly. Add the lye as slowly as you can bear and try to keep the mixture cool.

Check the temperature and when they are both around 115F you can combine them, stirring gently as you go, keeping your gloves and goggles on.

Using a stick blender, blend the mixture until it has reached an even consistency, with no globules of fat visible. If you want, you should add any essential oils or herbs at this point rather than later.

Pour into the receptacles of your choice and leave for at least 4 weeks. If you want to, you can cut it up after 24 hours into bars and things, but DO NOT TOUCH WITH SKIN FOR AT LEAST

4 WEEKS as soap burn, though it might seem ridiculous, is a real thing and can do you some very unpleasant damage.

Lotion

Homemade lotions are fun and easy to make. They are a great alternative for those with sensitive skin. Read any label on generic skin care and you will know how hard it is to find a product without a long list of ingredients. As a goat owner you will have access to a large amount of good quality goat's milk that you can use as and when you have a surplus.

You will need:
- 1 cup goat's milk
- 1/8 cup pure olive oil
- 1/8 tsp white vinegar (*acts as a natural preservative*)

Simply whisk the milk and oil together until it has formed a thick, creamy consistency. If you've ever made your own mayonnaise, you'll know that this can take a very long time, but once it's done you'll have a lovely consistency. Then mix in the vinegar to stop it going off.

You can add scented oils to add a little variety, but make sure that they're skin safe and that you're not sensitive to them. In an airtight jar, keep these lotions at room temperature for quite a long time, and if they separate out, simply re-mix them up again until they're back at a good texture.

Cajeta (caramel sauce)

Cajeta is Mexican caramel, made with slowly cooked sweetened milk (traditionally and preferably goat's milk) and infused with cinnamon, vanilla, or other spices and flavourings. Boer milk is especially good for this as it is sweet naturally.

You will need:
- 3 cups goat's milk
- 1 cup sugar
- 2 tsp corn syrup
- 1 cinnamon stick OR 1 TSP vanilla extract
- ¼ tsp baking soda dissolved in 1 tsp water

Mix together the goat's milk, sugar, corn syrup, and cinnamon stick in a very large pot (the mixture will swell as it cooks). Bring to a simmer over medium-high heat, stirring so the sugar dissolves.

Remove the pot from the heat and add the dissolved baking soda, stirring all the while. The mixture should froth, but if it doesn't, your goat's milk just might not be very acidic (that's okay). Stir it until most of the foam subsides.

Return the pot to medium-high heat and bring to a brisk simmer. Cook for an hour or so, or until the mixture turns golden. Stir every five minutes or so to make sure it isn't scorching on the bottom of the pan.

After the mixture turns pale golden, you'll need to start stirring more frequently. The mixture will darken to a caramel-gold colour and thicken to the regularity of golden syrup – it should easily coat the back of a spatula or spoon. This should take another 15 minutes or so, but you can continue to cook until it is the colour and thickness of your liking.

Strain the hot caramel mixture through a sieve into a container (preferably glass). Remove the cinnamon sticks from the sieve. (If you don't have a sieve, it's okay – you may find a lump or two in the finished caramel, and just make sure to remove the cinnamon sticks.)

The cajeta will thicken as it cools, and will keep in the refrigerator in a covered container for at least one month. If it is thicker than desired when cool, you can add warm or hot water to thin.

I recommend having some of this in the freezer for emergencies. And yes, there is such a thing as a sweet emergency.

Sticky toffee microwave cake (15 minute recipe)

This is a really easy dessert if you have unexpected dinner guests as it's very quick and relatively mess free (1 bowl, a whisk and a couple of silicone cake 'tins' are easily hidden under the washing up in our house!) It is also very impressive, as you can make it out of lots of your goat's milk ingredients. I first had this cake

when staying with friends who had goats and hens, and they used
their own eggs too, making me both impressed and jealous.
You will need:
- 3 eggs
- 6oz flour
- 6oz sugar
- 6oz butter (goat's butter works well)
- 2oz cajeta or toffee.

Put the wet ingredients, so eggs, butter and cajeta, into a bowl and
sieve the dry ingredients – flour and sugar – onto them. Whisk all
of the ingredients together. Separate into 2 silicone cake 'tins'.
Microwave each one separately for 2-3 minutes. -Once
microwaved, turn out of the cake 'tins' and leave to cool. This
whole process shouldn't take more than 15 minutes and is great if
you've forgotten cake for parties or school events. If you don't
have a microwave you can bake in a pre-heated 180 degree c oven
for 20 -25 minutes. DO NOT MICROWAVE METAL TINS.

Millionaire's goat's *cheesecake*
This is a really delicious dessert that never fails to impress. It's
rich, sweet, salty fatty flavours and textures are really quite
moreish and delicious.
You will need:
- 100g butter (goat's butter works well)
- 200g of soft goat's cheese
- 20g of cajeta
- 150g of chocolate
- ¼ cup goats milk

200g of digestive (sweetmeal) biscuits
Smash up the biscuits in a bowl with the end of a rolling pin. Melt
the butter in a Bain Marie or in a microwave on the defrost setting
and pour it into the mashed biscuits. Press this into a loose-
bottomed cake tin, or an ordinary high-sided cake tin lined with
cake paper.

As the base sets, whisk the cajeta and the cheese together until blended evenly. Then spread this over the base.
Melt the chocolate in the same way as the butter, being careful to mix and not let it burn.
Then add the goat's milk to the chocolate. At first, this will make the chocolate set but it will eventually be runny and smooth again so that you can pour it onto the top of the cheese cake (if you can't pour it at this stage it's ok, you can spoon it on).
Once cool, serve.

Chapter 8) Health

Goats are hardy and generally healthy animals. With proper nutrition and management, illness is rare. But of course, any living creature can get sick. You can do a lot to prevent sickness and injury. If your goats do fall ill, quick action can be the difference between life and death.

The health of your goats, as with any animals in your care, is not only a moral responsibility, but also a legal one. In the UK and the USA you can be prosecuted for having an untreated sick animal.

The way to avoid this is to keep an eye on the health of your animal, to keep up to date on vaccinations, and, importantly, to know what to look out for.

1. Vaccinations

There are so many illnesses that can damage the health of your goat that you need to do everything you can to avoid them. The easiest way to do that is to vaccinate. The four most common vaccinations for goats are tetanus, white muscle disease, Enterotoxaemia and Enterotoxaemia. You can also vaccinate for Chlamydia abortion, which kills unborn kids and causes early labour. Even though Boers have traditionally been bred to be robust, you still need to vaccinate as they can succumb to some horrid diseases.

Tetanus

Tetanus is a horrific illness, causing stiffness in joints, muscle rigidity, hyperesthesia and convulsions, often followed by a slow, painful death. It comes from microbes in soil, wood or metal that get into the blood through cuts and scrapes. If you are careful about hygiene and the animals your goats will meet, you might not need to vaccinate.

You can avoid this whole thing with a simple vaccination that is usually given as a single vaccination along with Enterotoxaemia.

The vaccine you want to use is CDT. You should vaccinate at the 4th month of pregnancy, 1 month old and then again at 2 months. From then on you should vaccinate every year if your animals are at risk of tetanus.

White-muscle disease

White-muscle disease is a degenerative illness that can be found in all large animals and is caused by a deficiency in selenium and/or vitamin E. As the name suggests, it affects the muscles, both skeletal and cardiac.

Symptoms that the skeletal muscles are affected are a real pain in walking and the muscles becoming stiff. The gait will be abnormal and the back may be arched. They'll become weak and listless.

Symptoms that the animal's cardiac muscles have been affected are like the symptoms of pneumonia. There will be difficulty breathing, snot and a fever. The heart rate will be irregular and fast, as will the breathing.

Treatments for white-muscle disease is not always affective, and animals that have had cardiac problems will rarely survive, and if they do, they certainly won't do well. Vaccinations are available though, and your vet will be able do advise you on them.

Enterotoxaemia

Enterotoxaemia, or overeating disease, is a very unpleasant illness that affects goats of all ages. It is caused by bacteria in the gut that overpopulates the gut, making the animal lethargic and causing stomach pain and diarrhoea.

The animal could stop being able to walk or stand. By the time the goat is struggling to stand it is too late and the poor thing will probably be dead in less than an hour. There is no real guaranteed treatment for this illness.

You can avoid this by good management and vaccinations, usually given as a single vaccination along with Enterotoxaemia. The vaccine you want to use is CDT, and will also protect your goats from tetanus as well. You should vaccinate at the 4th month of pregnancy, 1 month old and then again at 2 months. From then on you should vaccinate every year if your animals are at risk of enterotoxaemia. Your vet will be able to advise you about this.

Pasteurellosis
Pasteurellosis is an infectious disease infecting the blood and the lungs. It is a pneumonia-like illness that can kill your goat. Symptoms include vague depression and anorexia. There will be a little weight loss and listlessness. Breathing will then become difficult and weight loss with increase. The animal may cough and develop a snotty nose.

The prognosis for animals with pasteurellosis isn't good. In the later stages it doesn't respond well to antibiotics and the animal will probably die.

You can avoid this by good management and vaccinations. Your vet will be able to advise you about this.

Remember, vaccines are not cures: they're preventatives. You need to vaccinate before any illness is present and vaccinate regularly. This is where your logbook will come in handy.

Chlamydia abortion
Chlamydia abortion is a terrible thing for a doe. It can make her loose kids and stop her being able to carry to full term. The sad thing is that it can be prevented with a simple Chlamydia vaccine given between 28 and 45 days.

2. Illnesses and health problems

Pica
Pica is a psychological illness that makes animals crave non-food items. Goats aren't really prone to pica in the way that some people and dogs can develop it, but they do eat things that aren't food. This isn't an illness, per say, but it can cause some horrid problems.

As goats are bright and inquisitive, and as, like human children, they explore much of their world by putting things in their mouth, they can end up getting themselves into more trouble than other agricultural animals. You have to keep a real eye out for anything they can reach that can make them ill.

This includes non-digestible, non-food items, such as plastic and clothing. This can clog up in the gut, causing swelling and constipation. If enough rotting faecal matter backs up in any animal, it can be fatal.

Usually, goats don't eat non-food items unless they are starving, but they will often chew things up to see what happens and they can accidentally swallow things.

Obviously, you can't watch your goat all the time and there may be instances of a plastic grocery bag blowing into the pasture and being gobbled up without you noticing. What happens next, in these situations, can be the difference between life and death. Small amounts of plastic may be ground up in the stomach and passed with little or no consequence, but spotting the signs of a clog early means that your goat can be treated quickly.

If you suspect the goat has eaten something they shouldn't have, start watching out for excretions and any unusual behaviour, such as an achy stomach, irritableness, fever etc. I think I would give them mineral oil orally. Be careful though as they cannot taste mineral oil & they can aspirate it very easily.

If you follow this then you should never be in a position where a goat gets a big blockage of non-digestible substances in their gut. If this does happen, you will be able to feel that the abdomen is harder than usual. Your goat will become very irritable. The appetite will diminish.

Abortion

Abortions in goats will mostly occur from 6-8 weeks of pregnancy, and veterinary treatment is needed immediately to prevent infertility. You also need to make sure that the foetus is delivered as soon as possible so that it doesn't release toxins that will kill the mother too. Abortion could occur due to drinking water containing *salmonella typhinmurium*. Abortion can occur in a goat fed on rich clover or trefoil.

Acetonemia

Acetonemia, also called Ketosis Toxemia, is another horrid problem in goats – mainly pregnant does, caused by a lack of carbohydrates in the diet.

Symptoms include: loss of appetite, swelling legs, sluggishness and staggering/appearing drunk. If treated at this point there should be no development of the other symptoms, such as blindness, ataxia and coma. If the doe does fall into a coma, the foetuses will die inside the mother, releasing potentially fatal toxins into her.

At the first sign of any of these symptoms, add a high-energy supplement to the doe's diet, up the carbs, and start feeding "goat magic". Goat Magic is made from 1 part of molasses, 2 parts of Kayro Syrup, and 1 part of corn oil. You can adjust the amounts as long as you keep the proportions the same. Lots of goat owners keep a jar of this ready made up in case anything happens with their animals. Because it is made from all shed or housing ingredients, it will last for ages, as long as you keep it in a sealed container.

A good rule of thumb for avoiding this is to up the carbohydrate content of the diet when a goat is pregnant. The more kids you think she's carrying, the more carbohydrates she needs. You might even consider a spoon of goat magic in the daily feed.

If you're ever worried about your goat, whether you suspect you know what's wrong and you know how to treat it or not, you should seek veterinary advice.

Lice, fleas, mites and parasites

While many goats do not seem to get flees, there are some that are affected and you should keep an eye on your animals. If they do get fleas, they can be treated with capstar tablets or spot on. If using capstar to treat fleas, any milk should be discarded for 3 days after treatment. Capstar works by poisoning the fleas and the effect on milk are not positive. Do not stop milking the goat, as she will dry off. Goats can also get mites, lice and worms.

A heavy parasite burden can cause serious anaemia and with goats this can be fatal much quicker than with larger animals. Even if your goat survives a serious parasite burden, they could be left with some pretty horrific health problems as a result of organ damage. This is easily avoided, however, with the correct, regular preventative treatment and observation this can be avoided.

Mites, lice, ticks and other external parasites can be kept in check with regular grooming.

Goats need worming every 8 weeks. You can do this yourself with an oral de-wormer such as Ivermectin. If your goat is very young or stressed you should use a milder wormer or a daily wormer.

Diarrhoea

This can be caused by a number of things, including infections in the upper or lower gut and eating inappropriate foods or even a change in diet. Diarrhoea, whatever the underlying cause, can be fatal and any goat with diarrhoea should be given plenty of water with electrolytes. It causes rapid dehydration and you seek veterinary advice as soon as you notice any faeces that is loose or watery. Diarrhoea can kill much quicker than you might expect, as the salts and water lost are difficult to replace once the damage has begun.

If your goat has diarrhoea you need to keep their bedding scrupulously clean and be very aware of hygiene, as if an infection has caused the problem, the animal could accidentally re-infect itself.

Affected animals should be kept away from other animals to avoid further contamination. Your emergency kit should contain ProBalance or some pro-biotic and, oddly enough, liquorice. The pro-biotic should help to restore the lost gut flora and the liquorice should reduce digestive inflammation. You still need to see your vet about underlying causes. Seek veterinary advice.

Arthritis

Arthritis is a painful, progressive and limiting illness that affects many of us. It can also affect goats. The symptoms are fairly obvious and are decreased range of movement in less willingness to move about as much.

There are treatments that can alleviate the pain, though there is not yet a cure. If your goat develops arthritis, your vet will go through the various treatment options, and you should not consider arthritis the end of the animal's healthy life – they can still continue to have a good quality of life. The long-term prognosis for goats is better than that of larger animals. Because there is less weight on the joints and less pressure on the feet, they tend to suffer less if they do contract arthritis than other, larger livestock, such as cattle and Boers. This is a condition that can be managed in a way that doesn't affect the milk. Seek veterinary advice.

Anaemia

Anaemia is often a symptom of other problems and can be shown by a general paleness. The lips, guns and udder will be paler than usual and the goat may become lethargic. Anaemia is simply a lack of iron in getting to the goat, starving the cells of oxygen. It can be low iron in the blood, or low blood in the goat. Treatment can be done by the use of iron injection 5ml Dexavin (Pfizer) or Ferrofax (Duphar). Seek veterinary advice.

Rinderpest

Rinderpest is an acute, highly contagious disease caused by a Morbillivirus. In its acute form it is characterised by inflammation and necrosis of mucous membranes and a very high mortality rate. It is normally found in cattle, but has been known to cross into sheep and goats.

This is a notifiable disease and if you have an infected animal you need to contact the authorities. In the UK that's DEFRA and in the USA it's the department of agriculture.

Symptoms include mild thermal reaction and diarrhoea.

Ulcerative lesions appear on the inside of the lower tip and gums. Luckily, rinderpest is mostly found in Africa and is on the decline. If you do encounter an instance of this horrific illness, your animal will be destroyed and the carcass will need to be disposed of properly. Seek veterinary advice.

Anorexia

Though normally associated with young humans, anorexia can occur in any animal. The most important thing to find out is the cause. A loss of appetite could be voluntary Anorexia or Pathological Anorexia.

Symptoms include loss of appetite and weight loss. A milker will produce less milk and loose weight very rapidly. If there is a kid at foot, the kid may be adversely affected by this too. Contact the vet for advice and feed your animal up. Calf manna is a great way to help your goat put on weigh quickly.

Anthrax

That's right- anthrax. Like they try to steel/release in terrorist films. Anthrax is an acute disease caused by the bacterium *Bacillus anthracis,* which can survive all sorts of conditions and remain dormant in the ground until they find themselves in a host, where they will multiply and make animals horrifically ill. Symptoms include sudden high temperatures (108°F), loss of appetite, sudden death, and in a less acute form goat may live for a day and develop bloody diarrhoea.

You can avoid anthrax by keeping an eye on other animals that come into contact with yours and making sure that they are healthy. If you show or regularly move your goat, you should keep a record of where and when they have moved in the logbook. Keep the affected animal separate. Annual vaccination of goats in endemic area is recommended.

If you suspect anthrax, you need to contact DEFRA or the Department of Agriculture. It is a notifiable disease and the consequences for not notifying the authorities are severe. In fact, any sudden, unexplained deaths in your goat should be reported. There have been no cases of anthrax in the UK since 2006, but it can lay dormant in the ground and become a problem later.

Anthrax spores remain viable for decades in the soil or on animal products such as dried or processed hides or wool. Spores can survive for two years in water, 10 years in milk and up to 71 years on silk threads. You should check to make sure the land you're using has never had any cases.

Bronchitis
This occurs due to a lungworm infection or other infections causing damage to the lung.
Symptoms include coughing and listlessness.

Brucellosis
This is a horrid illness caused by *Brucella organisms.*
Symptoms include abortion in late pregnancy where retention of placenta and metritis are common. In male goats it causes infertility, orchitis and swollen joints. Goats should be tested for brucellosis and you have to isolate or cull the positive animals. Seek veterinary advice.

Big-Head
This is an acute, infectious disease, caused by bacteria. The disease is characterized by a rapid and unsightly swelling of the head, face, and neck, most commonly seen in young rams and bucks. This infection is initiated in young rams and bucks by their continual butting of one another. The bruised and battered subcutaneous tissues provide conditions suitable for growth of the bacteria, and the breaks in the skin offer an opportunity for their entrance.

Treatment may be possible with broad-spectrum antibiotics or penicillin if the disease is caught early. The disease may be prevented by vaccination against the bacteria involved.
Vaccinate pregnant ewes and does with a 7-way or 8-way vaccine during the last 30 days of pregnancy. The resulting high levels of antibodies in the colostrums should protect the lambs/kids.
Vaccinate lambs/kids with a 7-way or 8-way vaccine at 30 days

of age, and follow up with a booster in 2 to 4 weeks. In areas where disease has occurred, vaccination may be necessary every 6 months, though this could be less if you have better mannered animals or you don't have intact males living together. Seek veterinary advice about this one.

Bloat
Bloat is caused by a number of things, and can be a serious condition, which, if left untreated, can result in death to the goat. A build up of gas in the stomach and intestines caused by a rumen imbalance causes swelling, discomfort and occasionally ruptures. It can be caused by over eating and consuming too much fibre. It can be caused by too much pasture and weeds – they are quite good at only eating things that are good for them, but as they are greedy little so and sos, they sometimes eat weeds that can upset their tummies. A sudden change in diet can also cause bloat, especially if their regular diet doesn't have much variation in it. Symptoms include a distended (stretched out) abdomen, especially on the left side, an inability or unwillingness to move about and lying down a lot.

Treatment depends on the cause, which you can usually determine from looking back over your logbook. Have they gotten into the feed bins lately? Then it'll be an overeating problem. Has your goat been left out in a new pasture area or broken into a neighbour's garden? Then it's probably weeds. Has your grain supplier changed? hen the problem is probably caused by the diet change.

After working out what's caused the bloat, call a vet and if the goat can walk, walk them up and down a bit. Then give about a quarter of a pint of cooking oil and massage their sides. If the goat can release the gas on their own it will be a lot less invasive, so help them to move about and stretch. And wait for the vet. A little bicarbonate of soda and molasses is good for helping to relieve the bloat while you're waiting.

If the bloat is caused by weeds and the goat is likely to get out into the weeds again, leave a pan of bicarbonate of soda and molasses in some water with the goat to prevent it re-occurring. You can prevent a change of diet from causing bloat by always feeding the animal a good variety so that the digestion doesn't get lazy.

Cheesy Gland (CL)

This is a horrid illness that is also called yolk boils (Caseous lymphadenitis). This painful disease is caused by the bacterium coryne and bacterium pseudotuberculosis. It causes abscesses and boils that can be seen as swollen lumps under the jaw or on the neck. In goats, the head is most commonly affected, so the most likely point of entry of this infection is through cuts and scrapes on the head or in the mouth.

To avoid this illness, five different brands of cheesy-gland vaccines are available: Glanvac, cheesyvax, cydectin, Eweguard, Guardian and Websters 6-in-1.

To treat this illness, in goats with large abscesses, lance the abscess at the lowest point. Flush out the cavity with disinfectant after the pus has drained. Because pus is the main method of spread, it should be collected and disposed of safely by burying or treating with disinfectant. You should get a vet to show you this.

Obesity

Boer goats are far more prone to overeating than larger goats, and because of their stature, the relative weight gain is greater. Because of the smaller size of their gut, goats are only able to process small amounts of food at a time and so should be fed often, but only small amounts. Goats are less likely to get the exercise and restriction of access to pasture. Owners of larger goats can have real emotional niggles about feeding their minis so much less than everyone else. If your goat does become overweight, you need to seek veterinary advice before restricting the diet as there could be an underlying cause (other than gluttony).

Septicaemia

Septicaemia is a deadly bloodstream infection that can kill an animal very quickly. Septicemia is the presence of bacteria or bacterial toxins in the bloodstream, and can kill very quickly. As goats are smaller, they will succumb to the infection even faster than larger goats. The higher risk of death makes this a very serious illness and you need to be constantly on the lookout for septicaemia and seek veterinary advice as soon as you spot any signs, as early detection can literally be the difference between life and death. The younger the animal, the more danger it will be in, due to the weaker immune system. It is also far more likely in foals that have not had their colostrums.

There is no vaccination for this so you need to be very vigilant. It can often be treated with antibiotics, but not always, so prevention is the key. Any cuts, grazes or scrapes need to be treated with antiseptic cream and kept clean. This includes cuts in the mouth and splits in the hoof. Anywhere that any blood or flesh is in contact with the outside world, you need keep it clean. Unlike a lot of equine aliments, septicaemia isn't contagious by external contact.

3. Feet

Just like Boers and other hoofed animals, goat's hooves need regular trimming. In the wild these growths are kept under control by constant scrambling over rocks. Left untouched, overgrown hooves can cripple an animal by throwing bones out of alignment.

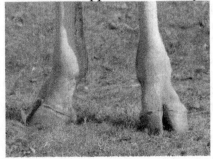

Hoof trimming can be accomplished with a sharp knife (and a great deal of care), but the ideal is a hoof trimmer and shears made for the purpose, available from goat and sheep supply houses. An alternative is ordinary sharp rose pruning shears. Leather gloves are a good idea. Most people will want to have a helper, or a milking stand to help restrain the goat.

Moving the leg back so the hoof faces up, first clean out any muck and dirt. Next trim off any bent-over parts of the hoof. It should be even with the bottom of the foot, but just take a little at a time until you gain experience. The hoof will show pink as you near the blood supply, so stop.
The toe, or point of the hoof, wears down less than the sides and requires more trimming. Heels seldom need trimming, but check them just in case.

Regular walking on hard surfaces may wear the hoof down and mean less hoof trimming, but you should keep an eye on the feet anyway.

4. Eyes

The eyes of a goat are very sensitive. All animals can get infections, disorders, and diseases of the eyes, including goats. Keeping the eyes clear of infections and diseases is important for the overall health of this unique animal. Cancers and tumours of the eyes can occur in goats. Keeping the eyes clean and knowing what your goat's eyes usually look like is very important and any changes in discharge or any damage should result in you seeking immediate veterinary attention.
Goats, like many animals, can be born with blindness. However, there are several diseases and illnesses that can lead to blindness and should be monitored closely. Poisoning from lead, pesticides, and some plants have lead to blindness. Diseases such as pregnancy toxemia and Vitamin A deficiencies can also cause blindness in goats. It is important to treat the underlying disease or illness before blindness occurs if possible.

5. Ears

Goat's ears need to be kept clean and clear from any mites and from infection. Any problems with the ear can transfer to problems elsewhere or could be symptomatic of other illnesses. As Boers have long, floppy ears, you should pay particular attention to them. They might try themselves to keep the ears clean of dirt, but their attempts will be clumsy and inaccurate. Take clean cotton wool to cloth and damp it with water and antibacterial spray or dip. Then gently clean any dirt or grease from the exposed part. Do not poke anything into the ear canal. Any unusual discharge from the ear should be checked out. Most goats will need to be marked and are usually marked by a coloured tag or a shaped hole. This needs to be done in absolutely sterile conditions to avoid infection.

6. Horns

Both male and female goats have horns. This female uses her horns to bully the other goats, especially when it's nearly time to kid. This is fine, as her horns are straight and don't get in the way, and the other goats in her pen generally keep out of her way anyway.
The issue with goats' horns is disbudding. It is a highly controversial one and can get you into all sorts of hotly debated arguments, whichever side you come down on.

Disbudding or de-horning is the removal of the horn buds in goat kids, and/or the removal of horns from adult goats, which can only be carried out by a veterinary surgeon in the UK.

The Royal College of Veterinary Surgeons considers the act of disbudding to be a mutilation, and as such requires serious thought before being undertaken, but it is accepted that for management and welfare reasons it is often necessary in larger goat enterprises.

As the horn bud grows extremely rapidly in goat kids, they should be disbudded between 2-7 days old, and must only be done by a vet with the kids under general anaesthesia +/- local nerve blocks.

Lots of people don't like disbudding because goat kids have very thin skulls and disbudding carried out by an untrained person can easily cause irreparable damage to the brain, either by direct heat transfer damage, or by facilitating the entry of bacteria into the skull, leading to a potentially fatal meningitis.

Many people argue that it's not really needed, especially if you're only going to have a couple of does. If you're having a few living together, having no horns can avoid serious injury.

The main advantage of having no horns is that they cannot grow back, towards the head. Ingrown horns will need major surgery and are unnecessarily painful. You can just cut the horns down as you go, filing away excess as they grow.

**Don't give your goat any medication without consulting your
vet** as this can cover up symptoms, meaning you could think your
goat has recovered. Keeping a logbook record of food and
behaviour may make it easier to pinpoint the cause and start of the
problem.

7. When to take your goat to the vet

A lot of little niggles and things that might worry your goat will
need treating, but not always by a vet. Most scrapes and scratches
and a little cold should be treated immediately to avoid infections,
but you can usually do this yourself. There are times, however,
when veterinary intervention is absolutely vital. There are also
times when it's hard to say- they might not *need* to see the vet but
it's always better safe than sorry.
A good rule of thumb is, when in doubt, seek veterinary advice.
Even if you've been told by friends or neighbours, or even books,
that you don't need to see a vet, if you are unsure, phone them.
They may reassure you over the phone that it's fine, or they may
come out and save the goat's life.

Becoming unresponsive
If, for any reason that you know of, or if you can't work out why,
your goat becomes unresponsive you must seek veterinary advice

as soon as possible. Not responding to noise can suggest ear infections, deafness or head trauma. Ignoring the sight and movement of those around it can suggest any number of illnesses, including infections, problems with eyesight and physical distress.

Thirst or hunger

Excessive thirst or hunger can be a sign of all sorts of horrid things, such as poisoning, diabetes and infections. Don't panic immediately though. The first thing that you need to check is whether or not your goat has had access to enough clean water. If not then that could explain why they are so thirsty. If they have not had access to water for some time you may still want to consult your vet, as dehydration can make animals very poorly. But if there was sufficient water and they drank it all, and continued to be thirsty, this could mean your animal is unwell. Seek veterinary advice.

Poison

If your goat has ingested something you know or even suspect to be poisonous, or even if you only think they may have, you must seek veterinary advice immediately. If the poison is not corrosive or irritant you may be able to help by inducing vomiting. You should only do this if your vet has okayed it and you know that it is safe. There are a number of ways to do this, but salt is the best way.

Seizure

If your goat has any sort of seizure, no matter how small, go to the vet. A seizure can look like a small, sudden collapse that seems quickly recovered from, or it can be a collapse followed by a worrying time of incapacity and possibly shaking. It can also be very subtle, with all of the muscles tensing up and the goat becoming rigid. Most animals suffering from a seizure will evacuate their bowels. If you suspect a seizure, seek veterinary advice.

Strange movement

If your goat begins to move strangely and you can't see a reason; for example if they aren't used to being tethered, to seek veterinary advice. Strange movements can be an indication of neurological problems, or it could be an early indication of narcolepsy. Strange movements can also be associated with physical discomfort. A goat with arthritis, tetanus or any bone or muscle damage will need treating immediately. It could also just be a hoof that needs cleaning better, so make sure you check the possibilities.

Fur loss

Fur loss is often indicative of a lice infestation or poor health and condition. If you are confident that your goat does not have any external parasites, you should seek veterinary advice for both treatment of the fur loss and the underlying cause.

Lumps and bumps

If you feel an abnormal lump, it isn't necessarily cancer, but you need to seek immediate veterinary help, as even a benign fat lump can make your goat uncomfortable or ill. Other lumps may be fluid trapped underneath the skin; this is called dependent edema and could be a sign of arthritis, a very serious illness. Any bruises should be looked at and the cause of any bruising should be investigated and, where possible, removed.

Bleeding

Any profuse bleeding, obviously, needs to be seen by the vet. A little scratch will usually be ok, but even a small cut can become infected and an infection needs to be treated by the vet before septicaemia sets in. You should have an antiseptic rub in your emergency kit. If a small cut takes a long time to heel, you can treat it with styptic. You should also have styptic in your emergency kit.

Broken bones

This is very obvious but any serious injury or wound of any kind needs veterinary help. If you even suspect any broken bones, your goat needs urgent veterinary attention.

Discharge from the eyes or nose
This could be a symptom of a serious respiratory illness, or just a little sniffle. It's always better safe than sorry and if your goat does have a respiratory infection the sooner it is treated the better. If any discharge continues for more than a couple of days, is excessive, contains any blood or is coupled with any other symptoms you should seek veterinary advice.

Don't give your goat any medication without consulting your vet as this can cover up symptoms, meaning you could think your goat has recovered. Keeping a logbook record of food and behaviour may make it easier to pinpoint the cause and start of the problem.

8. Emergency kit
There are a few things you should have on hand with any pet. With most pets you can get the things you'll need in an emergency quite readily at a local store or supermarket. Goats, however, are not very common pets, and should the occasion arise, there are a few things you should have in case of an emergency. An animal first aid kit is an old idea, but a good one. You will need:
- Styptic
- Antiseptic
- Electrolyte compound
- Probiotics
- Salt

Styptic
Styptic is a clotting agent used by all sorts of people for all sorts of reasons. Men use it when they cut themselves shaving; rabbit owners use it when they cut the claws too short. When sprinkled

on small cuts that bleed for too long, styptic is a fantastic clotting aid and can help a wound heel quickly, avoiding infection. It comes in stick form for human use, but is also available as a powder, such as Kwik-Stop Styptic Powder and works out at about $10 or £7 an ounce. Most goat owners won't use anywhere near that in an animals lifetime.

Antiseptic
An antiseptic gel like Radiol B-R antibacterial Jelly or a spray like Purple Spray can help avoid all sorts of problems. Applied directly and immediately to any minor cuts, scrapes and grazes, an anti-bacterial agent can stop infections occurring, potentially saving hundreds, if not thousands in veterinary bills, as well as a lot of pain and distress for your goat. Any infections should be treated immediately by the vet to avoid septicaemia, and any real wounds need to be looked at by a vet anyway.

Electrolyte compound
Keeping a compound of electrolytes handy could well save your goat's life if they ever develop any diarrhoea or dehydration. If there is ever any point at which your goat is ill they could easily become dehydrated and die of dehydration rather than the initial illness.

Probiotics
Because of the complex nature of goat digestion, it is important that their gut flora is kept healthy. If there has been any problem with digestion, whether it is sudden weight loss or just a small bout of diarrhoea, replacing the 'good' bacteria and promoting its health in the animal's gut is vitally important.

Salt
There are some very specific circumstances when it is necessary to induce vomiting. This should only be done under veterinary instruction. Salt is the safest way to do this.

9. *Administering medical help*

There are a number of things you might need to do to administer medical help to your goat. This is a guide or memory jogger only, and you should ask your vet to show you what to do.

Injections

If you decide to administer your own vaccinations, make sure you know what you are doing. Ask your vet to show you how. There are 2 types of injection that you may need. The most common, easiest and useful is subcutaneous. The other type is intramuscular.

To fill your syringe, fit a new, clean, disposable needle to the syringe and draw the medication into the syringe. Tap the side of the syringe to make sure there are no air bubbles, and close the plunger to remove the air and let out any excess liquid.

Subcutaneous injections can be given easily by lifting the skin into a sort of tent. You can practice this now to see what I mean by pinching up the skin on the back of your hand. You can find loose skin like this on your goat to inject behind. Then push the needle into the skin towards the body, making sure you don't stick the muscle or any veins. Then push the plunger to release the vaccine.

Intramuscular injections are a little riskier. You need to push the needle into the muscle, making sure you avoid bone and nerves. You can avoid nerves by avoiding the hind legs.

Inducing vomiting

Inducing vomiting should not be done lightly. Only if your goat has ingested large amounts of poisonous plants that are not corrosive or irritant, and under veterinary instruction, should you induce vomiting. You do this by pouring 2 tablespoons of table salt onto the back of the tongue. Then you must keep the mouth closed until the salt is swallowed. Keep your goat company and as calm as you can.

Pills

Pills can be administered by opening the mouth and popping them onto the back of the tongue, or by hiding them among a handful of treats.

Chapter 9) Play and enrichment

Goats are intelligent animals and are easily bored. A bored animal is an unhappy animal, and as an owner it is your responsibility to keep your goat happy. You can't be with them all of the time, but you can and should provide entertainment.
Most fields don't have mountains or cliffs for goats to exercise their natural behaviours, so you need to provide some way for them to do that. Bored goats can become destructive and aggressive.
Even a pile of logs, a bale of hay or a little wall will be appreciated.

There is a wide range of toys available to keep goats occupied. A lot of these toys will involve a food treat. You can use this as an opportunity to give your goat some much needed dietary supplements. You can get toy compatible treats that contain all sorts of things, from salt licks to cod-liver oil. Many owners also use these treat toys to administer wormer and other medications.

Goats love toys; they will make toys of all sorts of things that they find. You can't be with them all day every day, and even the best animal company doesn't always provide the entertainment and enrichment your goats will need.

1. Bought toys

There are lots of websites that sell boredom busters for goats. These clever companies make all sorts of food-based enrichment toys that can keep your goat entertained when you're not around.

Hanging likit holder

There are all sorts of hanging holders for salt licks and treats out there. They are a fantastic way to keep your goat entertained and healthy, as you can use them to introduce electrolytes, vitamins and other dietary supplements. These devices hang from the ceiling and contain delicious things that are good for your goat and that they want to lick. Because it is hanging, it moves around and the goat will have to move their head and neck about to taste and bite their treat. This provides a nice bit of mental exercise.

Tongue twister

The tong twister is a similar thing to the hanging holder, but it can be attached to the shed or housing wall or to fence posts and trees. It holds the treat and the goat has to twist their tongue around to get at it. The device doesn't move about but its components do, moving and getting in the way of the enquiring tongue and making the goat think and move about.

Boredom Breaker

This is a clever hanging toy with a hanging lickit holder and a ball suspended from the bottom of the string. The ball has a compartment for more treats and because the ball turns round, the treats aren't always at the front for the goat to access, so the goat has to use their mind a bit to get at their treat.

Treat balls

The Snak-a-ball (http://www.likit.co.uk/) or Pasture Pal (http://www.equi-spirit-toys.com) or Nose-It (http://www.nose-it.com) are very similar to treat balls for smaller animals and can be filled with whatever feed you use for your goat. It rolls around on the ground and the goat nudges it to move it about. The food falls out of the hole in small amounts for the goat to eat. This is excellent because not only does it keep your goat occupied, it also keeps the food relatively clean while encouraging natural grazing behaviours, which have a beneficial effect on the mental wellbeing of animals in captivity.

Balls

There is a whole range of balls for goats to play with, from traditional footballs (soccer balls) to balls with handles that they can carry about with them. The amazing thing is, that goats will play with these with very little encouragement, and if left alone with them, will play with them whenever they want entertainment. It's a special joy that you get from watching a goat playing with a ball, kicking and nosing it about the paddock.

2. Home made toys and how to make them

Things with the word "goat" in front of them will often come with a high price tag, but that doesn't mean you can't keep your goat entertained without breaking the bank. There are all sorts of toys you can make yourself or adapt from other things that will keep your goats happy and entertained.

Ice-lolly

On very hot days, your goat needs to keep cool. A good way to help them do this is to chop up some of their favourite fruits and veggies and freeze then in a block of water. Old ice cream or margarine tubs make good ice trays and make ice-lollies of about the right size. Ice should only be given on very hot days and only in small amounts. It should also be supervised. I'm not saying stand there and watch until it's all eaten up, but someone should be around if your goat is being given a frozen treat to cool down in case the weather changes.

Hay hanger

If you hang your hay in hay nets, try suspending them from the rafters so that the goat has to work at getting the hay out as the bundle moves and sways.

Obstacle course
Goats love to climb. It's obvious really, but they really do love to clamber about. Having lots of things for them to climb on is essential stimulation for a goat. It's also very entertaining to watch. An obstacle course can be made from anything that won't hurt them. Upturned boxes and buckets to clamber on and cargo nets hung about for them to wriggle under will create hours of play. Mounds of dirt, even, will be greatly appreciated, and they will clamber about playing king of the castle.

Seesaw
That's right. Many goats love a seesaw. A barrel with a plant tied to it will provide hours of fun, and when they're done playing on the seesaw they'll enjoy nibbling on the rope.

Dinner hanger
Hanging their food is a great way to keep your goat entertained while they are indoors overnight. There are lots of ways to do this, but wrapping the regular feed up with a few treats and binding it in hay is a great way to do it. If you bind the hay tight with jute or hemp, the food will be bound up and difficult to get at, providing a little extra challenge with dinner.

Bobbing for apples
All you need of this is a large water container barrel and some apples. This is a really fun game for your goat; they can search around for ages and can be left to play with this on their own.

Home made feed-ball
Goats love to kick things about and you can use any large container such as a 2-litre drinks bottle or a gallon milk bottle to make your own feed-ball. If you drill a few holes in the side and leave the lid off, you can fill the container with treats and leave the lid off to avoid choking. Your goat will love kicking this about

and foraging for the tasty things that escape.

Grazing roller
Or you can tie hay around a drainpipe with strong jute or hemp string. Wrap a lot round and tie great big handfuls of it on. Then you can leave it with your goat to graze from. This way, it will roll out of reach, making your goat work a little harder for their dinner.

Hanging bottle treat
Or, if you choose, you can make a treat bottle in the same way, with holes on the bottom or with the lid left off and hung up side down. The goat will have to really work at it to make the treats come out. They will have a real time wriggling out their treats or food.

Play rope
It could be as easy and simple as a plastic milk jug, you can find some nice hard rubber dog toys, or even plastic bowls of different shapes or colours. The ideal height depends on the goat's height. You would want to hang it such that the hanging item can just touch his back. My guys love to walk under some of the toys to try and scratch their backs & others like to pull on it. Some days you don't want to hang anything. The idea is to keep it interesting & see what you can come up with that is relatively safe.

Kick bottle
Bottles filled with treats make great kick toys. Just leave the lid off to avoid any risk of chocking on it and to let some of the treats come out. This should release the food only after some effort and scatter it randomly, encouraging natural foraging and grazing behaviour. You can use these to feed all of your goats in the winter when your goats are kept in.

Rummage box
A rummage box is a spectacular idea for a goat toy. Take an old

draw or something similar and fill it with largish, smooth pebbles so no noses or tongues get grazed. Then just pop in pieces of apple/treats in amongst the pebbles and the goat spends quite a while working his mouth around the pebbles to find the treats.

Paper bags / cardboard boxes

This isn't technically a made toy or even really a toy, but goats of all sizes love paper bags and scrunched up newspaper to make a game of. They toss them in the air and chase them and tear at them and have such fun! Other types of packaging such as boxes with any staples and tape removed are used much the same, but will last quite a bit before they have been torn up completely.

Willow branches

Willow branches make great chews for goats. They absolutely love willow. Goats know what's good for them and willow kills worms and thins the blood, which stops it building up in the hooves. Thinner blood doesn't clog in the tiny capillaries in the hooves, reducing the likelihood of laminitis. Not only is willow good for your goat, but they love it too. Willow makes both a medicine and a treat for lots of animals. Many horse riders include a willow stop on their route.

You can buy most of these things on eBay, but you can also pick these things up at supermarkets, second hand shops and scrap yards.

Chapter 10) Training your goat

Training your goat is a great way to spend time with them, to bond with them, and to save time and energy when it comes to doing routine things like cleaning out the feet, or unusual things like catching them for vet checks. And it can be done. Just look on YouTube for videos of clicker-trained goats doing all of their tricks and showing off.

The key to training any animal is perseverance, but it is obvious from watching the goat wiggling its tail that they enjoy their games. Lots of positive reinforcement and the opportunity to exercise their brains and show off make training a great enrichment activity for goats.

The problem a lot of people have when it comes time to train their goat is that they don't want to give too many treats and make their goat ill or fat. This is where techniques you'd use for dog training come in. That's right – clicker training! You can teach a goat to do almost anything with clicker training.

You need a clicker, which is a mechanical device that makes a click sound, and treats such as peanuts or flakes of cereal. By combining the click with a treat, you reinforce that the goat is doing the right thing. You need to start by getting the goat to make a connection between the clicker and a treat. To do this, click the clicker and then give the goat a treat about 20 to 30 times. Your goat begins to associate the clicker with food and eventually the clicker sound will be married up with the pleasure sensation from the treats in the animal's brain. You can trick the brain chemistry to release the same chemicals that make them enjoy food when the clicker noise happens.

Coming When Called
Give your Boer goat its clicker treat while saying its name over and over again. Do this daily to reinforce the training. Make sure

that when the Boer goat comes to you, you do reward it each and every time.

When they come towards you, say their name again in a slightly higher register and when they get to you, give them the treat. Then when they wander off again, call them. If they make the connection quickly, they will come to you very quickly.Each time the goat comes to you, say their name again and give the treat and a big fuss. Once the goat has got the hang of this, get someone to hold them, not too far away. Then, when the goat is released, call them until they do, and give them the treat. Then try it from further and further away, giving lots of praise and strokes and fuss as well as the treat each time they do it right. This should come quite quickly to most goats, but with some it may need a bit of persistence.

Biting

If your Boer goat gets into a habit of getting what they want by biting you, they will continue to do so. If you pull away when your goat bites, then they will think they are in charge. They need to know that no one is in charge, but that no one is submissive. Goats are herd animals and in a herd there is a pecking order. Biting can be a very worrying problem. Let's say you love your goat but they have begun to bite and you know how dangerous this can be. This isn't the end of the world if you nip it in the bud (no pun intended). A few simple rules will keep you out of such a situation, but if you are very worried about biting, never be afraid to call on professional help.

The main thing to do if your goat bites is to understand *why* they have bitten. Could it be that they were just showing affection? In the wild, goats nibble at the top of each other's neck to show affection. Is it because they have been spooked by something and they are trying to get your attention or comfort? Or are they genuinely being aggressive?

If they are trying to show affection, you need to show them a more appropriate way. Teach them to show affection by nuzzling instead.

If they are spooked, out a firm hand on their neck and show them that they are safe. If they are being aggressive, you need to be firm. Put your hand on their nose and push their face down –not so hard or firm as to hurt them, just enough to let them know that you won't stand for that sort of behaviour. Stand up straight and show them that you are bigger. It is important that you do not loose your temper at any point. If you loose your temper and make your animal afraid of you, it can take a very long time to regain their trust once you have broken it.

Showing hooves

Teaching your goat to be calm and stand still while you inspect each hoof will save time and reduce stress when it comes to checking and trimming hooves.

Firstly, calm your goat, and stand next to them, still and firm. If there is anyone with you, ask him or her to calm your goat at their face, feeding them treats and cooing. If there is no one with you, stand your goat by their food trough, so that they are distracted and calm. The main event shouldn't be their feet being lifted and checked. If the most important thing that is happening is the food, that is what they will care about. Hold the foot for a very short time at first, increasing the time as you go on. If you normalize the foot inspection by repeating this action as often as possible, then when the time comes to have the hooves rasped, cleaned out or trimmed there will be no fear involved.

Sit

Goats can be trained to sit much in the same way as dogs. Teaching your goat to sit is relatively easy, especially if you have a particularly food centered goat. Let the goat know that you have the treat. Let them know it's in your hand. Stand upright in front of the goat. Put the treat on your hand, palm up and move it above their head. The goat should automatically sit. When they do, say "sit" and give them the treat and a fuss. If they walk backwards instead of sitting, you could get someone to stand behind the goat. Repeating this whenever possible, without tiring out the goat, will mean they learn this very quickly. If the goat seems to be struggling with this, you can put a little light pressure on the back as you give the command. Do not push the goat's back down – this could not only hurt the goat, but break the trust. Training is about trust.

Lie down

Lie down, while not necessary, can be a really useful command to be able to give under some circumstances. With this method, you need to have already taught "sit". Get the goat to sit, but do not give the treat – keep it in your hand. Then point to or tap on the floor below the goat's nose as they are sitting. The goat should lie down.

If they don't, you can apply a small amount of pressure on the shoulders, but not much. If you hurt your goat it will resent training and probably you. As I've already said, training is about trust. Once the goat lies down, say "lie down" and give the treat. Then, after doing this for a while, you can try saying the command and pointing before the goat lies down. Once they've got the hang of this, stand up and do the whole thing from standing until the goat has learned the trick.

Shake hoof

This is a very useful trick to teach your goat, as it will make keeping the hooves clean and short a lot easier. You can teach your goat to shake hands. It is easier to do this once the goat has learned to sit. Once the goat is sitting, take their front leg and give whatever command you've chosen. Then give the treat or the click. Keep doing this until the goat can remember to give the hoof on command before you take the hoof. Remember to reward every time they get it right.

You can also teach your goat to dance around in circles, walk backwards and to jump onto and off things, using those techniques.

Chapter 11) Breeding

It is now thought best to leave goats until 14-18 months of age before having them served or covered. The gestation period is approximately 5 months. Mating earlier than this age is possible but undesirable. Male kids should be separated from females at 10 weeks of age. Kiddings are usually uncomplicated, but it is advisable for owners to be present. Kids may be weaned at 12-14 weeks if they are taking a good ration of concentrates, but left with their mothers they may continue to suckle for seven months or more.

As your goat is probably a dairy animal and you probably have her for milk, you will, obviously, be breeding from her. You will usually buy a goat that is in milk and then have to breed her once she runs dry, avoiding the drama of breeding until you are familiar with your doe.

If you own a male that is strong and healthy and are interested in hiring him out to stud, there is little to stop you. You should really get seek and recognize advice from current goat breeders who have an excellent reputation with other Boer breeders; check with your local Boer association for more information. Most breeders will be happy to share information, as they're as keen as you to maintain high quality standards and to see more healthy goats.

1. Preparation

There are no different housing requirements, but you should be extra vigilant about hygiene and making sure the shed is cleaned out and free from anything that might damage a new baby kid. In case anything goes wrong, you should have some colostrums in the freezer. This will allow you to get baby the immune protection it needs as soon as possible if, for any reason, the mother can't feed the kid.

2. Mating

If you've not got much experience with goats you really shouldn't attempt breeding at home. Take your doe to an experienced goat owner for stud.

Does can be bred when they weigh 85-90 pounds, usually at about nine months of age, but most people consider that you should wait a little longer than this and have the doe health checked before any breeding goes on.

Female goats are only receptive to breeding ("in heat" or oestrus) for 2-3 days at a time, every 18-23 days or so, usually from fall to late winter. Signs to watch for include increased tail wagging, nervous bleating, a slightly swollen vulva, and frequent urination. Take the doe to visit the buck, record the date in your log, and watch for signs of heat again about three weeks later. If you see none, the doe is probably pregnant.

Again mark your calendar, anticipating kidding about 145 to 150 days after breeding.

3. Pregnancy

You should make sure mum has a lot of good quality feed, extra grain and constant access to water. She will also need somewhere to keep warm and dry if the weather turns.

As soon as you know the doe is expecting, you should be observing her more closely.

About 50-100 days into the pregnancy you should stop milking (if you haven't already) and let her dry off. At this point she'll wean any kids that she still has at foot, anyway.

At 115 days, make sure she has enough vitamin E and selenium, and if you live in an area where the ground is deficient in these, give her a shot; your vet can advise you on this.

At 120-125 days give Enterotoxaemia & Tetanus vaccine; again, your vet will be able to advise you on this.

When your doe is 130 days pregnant start adding vitamin E to the feed to make sure your kid is getting enough.

From day 140 onwards you should be ready for baby to arrive any day.

Keep your fingernails short and clean – this isn't something you'll remember to do when the time comes, so just be prepared.

Shave her tummy and around her parts so that you can keep an eye on any movement. It also makes it easier to clean her up after the birth.

Start keeping her in the stall where she will be giving birth. If you only have 2 goats, just make sure their regular stall is clean and tidy. If you have a few, put her in a separate, clean stall with her 'best' friend- an animal she never fights with and who will keep her calm. This means that when the time comes being somewhere strange when she is in labour won't freak her out.

4. Kidding

Several days ahead of the due date, put the doe in a well-cleaned pen by herself with plenty of fresh bedding, water, and good hay. Don't be surprised if you check on her one morning and find her tending to 2-3 newborn kids, even if you didn't know she was in labour.

At the onset of labour she might paw the floor and lie down and stand again repeatedly. If she is in actual labour more than two hours or seems to be having trouble, be ready to call for help from either a knowledgeable neighbour or a veterinarian. You should know in advance whom you're going to call. The best way to learn to deal with rare, difficult births is by watching someone with experience.

The normal procedure after kidding is to clear the nose of mucus or membranes to prevent suffocation (the mother will do this if you aren't there), disinfect the navel with iodine, and dry the kid. Gently draw a small stream of milk from each teat to be sure it's functional and not plugged. Clean up the soiled bedding and add fresh, if needed. Watch to be certain the kids get that all-important first drink of "colostrums," or first milk, or milk the doe and feed the kids with a bottle and lamb nipple. This thick, yellowish milk produced for the first few days after giving birth is essential for any newborn.

5. *Bringing up baby*

There are many theories of kid raising, most related in some way to why you raise goats. The "natural" way would be to leave them with their mother. Many believe that this won't work if you're raising goats for milk. Kids can ruin udders on show goats. And concerns about certain diseases (CAE) lead many goat raisers to remove kids from their mothers immediately after birth.

Be sure to provide fine-stemmed hay available to the kid, which kids will start nibbling at when they're only a week old. This roughage is essential for the proper development of the stomach and rumen. They will nibble at grain (18% kid ration) soon after, but the hay is more important. Limiting feeding milk at this point will encourage hay and grain consumption, but always offer as much clean water as they will drink.

Wean by weight, not age, usually around 20 pounds. The primary consideration should be whether they are consuming enough hay and grain to continue to thrive without milk.

If you take the kid away, you'll need to feed it with mum's milk. You can get special lamb bottles to do this with. If at all possible, make sure the kid gets the first milk or colostrums. Colostrums provide valuable antibodies, which protect the kid for the first several weeks of life. After this, the kid's own body starts producing its own antibodies. The only time colostrums should not be fed is if the doe has the disease CAE, or is suspected of having this disease. It is then vital that the kid drinks absolutely no milk from its mother, as CAE is passed on through the milk.

Feed kids 3 to 4 times daily for the first 2 weeks of life. We feed kids 3 times a day for the first month, 2 feeds a day for the second month, and 1 feed a day for the third month. Boers will happily drink about a litre of milk per day, so divide this up between feeds. Remember to feed small amounts at a time, as too much milk can drown the kid if its lungs overflow.
NEVER BOTTLE FEED A COLD KID. Make sure that they are warm and active before feeding, or they could drown.
Offer water and hay for the kid to pick at from the first week of life. The sooner the kids begin eating concentrates the sooner they can be weaned off milk. Concentrates can include high protein calf pellets, oats, barley, dairy meal or high protein horse feeds.

Aim at weaning the kids by 12 weeks of age unless you have plentiful supplies of milk, or need to push its growth quickly.

Another option here is to have 2 mothers, one bringing up the kids and the other for milking.

Insurance
One thing you need to take into account is that your insurance may be invalidated by a pregnancy. You'd need to contact your insurer to find out where you stand. They might have a special

pregnancy cover, but they might not. Just not telling the insurance company isn't really an option as someone would notice. Your insurance may be affected for some time after the birth as well. Most goat insurance will cover pregnancy as they are generally kept as dairy animals.

Dangers
There are all sorts of infections that can kill the foetus before it is even born. A dead foetus in the uterus can release toxins that can kill the doe. A pregnant doe can become erratic and her behaviour may change permanently. Pregnancy of young does can hinder their growth, so you need to make sure your doe is old enough and big enough. Coming into heat isn't necessarily a sign that she is physically prepared to have a baby.
Multiple kids- twins or triplets – can weaken the doe a lot and you need to make sure that your doe has access to enough quality feed to avoid illness.
A prolapsed uterus can kill a goat very easily, and you should have a vet look at your doe to check her over, as it could take up to 3 weeks of care to nurse her back to health, and without this she could die.
As Boers they are essentially prey animals, they tend not to advertise any potential problems.
Any number of complications in pregnancy or birth could do some real damage, or even kill both mother and foal.

Legal ramifications
You are legally responsible for the kid even before they are born, and you are legally required to provide adequate care for them.

Looking after mum and baby
Keeping the nutrition high and the wind out is the main thing you can do to keep mum and baby safe and healthy. You should watch the baby. They should be on their feet and feeding within 2-3 hours. The mother will be very attached to them very quickly and

should provide any care they need.

If the kid is early, struggling to breathe, took more than 40 minutes to birth, the mare won't allow the baby to nurse or they take longer than 3 hours to be born, they may well be in trouble. At this point you need to call your vet for help.

6. What to do if the mother rejects the babies

If your Boer rejects her baby, you need to act fast. Without the protection of their mother, the foal could die very quickly. Try to reintroduce the foal. If this fails, or if your doe dies in labour, contact all of the Boer breeders you can. Try to find a lactating doe to foster the baby. They will often take another mare's foal if the foal is abandoned.

If you cannot find another doe to feed your kid, you need to keep them as warm as possible. Luckily, goat's milk is quite easy to get hold of. Any friendly farmer or goat breeder should be able to help you get hold of goat's colostrums in an emergency, but if you've prepped properly you should have some in the freezer. The milk should be warmed but not burnt and cows milk is not appropriate, even, as some claim, so called 'scolded' cows milk. This will make little kid tummies very upset. So you have your warm goat's milk, in the bottle. Always feed your Boer standing up, if they are lying down they may drown. Kids to be hand-fed should be placed in a well-bedded, draft-free box, preferably out of sight and hearing of the mother. They can be fed from bottles or pans. It requires time and patience to teach a kid to drink from a pan, but cleaning and sanitizing bottles and nipples is more work.

Most people feed warmed milk (a goat's normal body temperature is 103°) three or four times a day. Start with 12-14 ounces a day the first few days, working up to as much as 24 ounces a day by the end of the week, if the kid will take it. Some won't. If your kid isn't taking as much as this – don't panic. As long as they are taking almost this much, and are bright and alert, then they should be fine. By the second week this will probably increase to 36 ounces a day.

If you're worried, contact a vet. There is also loads of advice about this on forums and people will be happy to help you.

NEVER feed a baby if it is cold. This can kill the kid, putting all your hard work and heartache to waste.

Chapter 12) Showing goats

One reason an increasing number of people keep Boer goats is nothing to do with milk or breeding at all. It is all about showing. The breed standard for Boer goats is fairly relaxed about coat colours and markings, though some judges prefer the traditional white body with red facial markings, but body type, coat length, temperament and health will all be taken into account when showing and competing.

Before entering your goat in any shows, you should attend a few to see what the atmosphere and expectations are like. You can see what judges are looking for first hand and speak to knowledgeable owners who can let you know what to expect from first hand experience.

Goat shows are a real barrel of laughs usually, but competing owners can be very fussy about some things – touching or petting other people's goats, feeding other people's goats, even taking photographs of other people's goats – can really land you in hot water if you aren't careful. Make sure you know the specific etiquette of each event before you do anything.

The head, neck and legs should be short in relation to body length. The body is full-barrelled or 'stocky' and well muscled, circumference in relation to height and weight is proportionally greater than in other breeds. Sexual characteristics are clearly defined. Females are considered mature at 24 months, males at 30 months, although some animals may continue to grow after this age.

Head
Short to medium long, convex Roman nose, well-rounded muzzle with full chin and even bite. Forehead should be broad, flat to convex. If you are showing your goats then the head should be red or red with a small white blaze, no more.

Eyes
Eyes should be set well apart, bright, dark and soft but not protruding or staring.

Ears
Ears should be medium long, clean and floppy. They should be smooth and broad. The ears of a Boer goat should be diamond shaped. If you are to show your goats, the ears should be all red, but some white is permissible.

Horns
Genetically, your goat will be horned. The males have stronger horns than the wethers and the females. If you are showing your Boers, they should have horns or disbudding permissible. Horns, if present, must be symmetrical.

Mouth
The mouth should have a good form with the teeth meeting the upper dental pad.

Coat
The full coat of straight hair that is short and glossy. There won't be any beard. The coat should be a clean.

Neck
Boars have short, thick, well-muscled necks. If you're showing your goat, it can be red or white.

Shoulders
The shoulders are broad and strong. If you are showing your goat then only the front and tops should be red, the colour should not extend further back than the shoulder blades.

Legs
Strong, well muscled, wide apart. Forelegs; proportionately short, straight, wide apart and squarely set with elbows close to ribs.

Cannon bone short. Hind legs (viewed from rear) straight, widely set, hocks cleanly moulded, sharply angled. Pasterns short, strong and resilient. Feet well shaped with deep heel and level sole.

Body Capacity
Large in proportion to size of animal, providing ample digestive and reproductive capacity, strength, vigour and stamina. Barrel broad and deep, increasing in width towards flank, giving an impression of perpetual pregnancy, symmetrical and well supported by firm abdominal wall and well-sprung ribs.

Back
The back of the Boer is strong, broad and straight. The loin should be wide, well muscled and strong.

Rump
Medium long, medium wide, neither level nor steep. Hips wide, nearly level with the back. Pin bones wide apart, somewhat lower than hips.
Pronounced tail, set high, wide at base, held straight.

Mammary System
Udder firm, rounded, small to medium size. Teats placed symmetrically, free from multiple or deformed teats and multiple orifices.

Colour
For show purposes, a Boer should usually have a read head and white body.
Colour is permissible only on the neck and forequarter, limited to the shoulder blades and not lower down on the shoulder than level to where the forearm joins the chest.
There may be a white blaze on the face, but the face should be symmetrical and predominantly red. Both ears should be at least 75% red.

115

Some red of no more than 10cm diameter is permissible on the barrel, back or hindquarters. The tail may be red, but the red can't continue onto the body.

Males should have an obviously masculine head with the neck and shoulders not showing any trace coarseness. Horns longer and sturdier than those of the female. Disbudding is allowed in show animals. The barrel (tummy) may be slightly less well developed than the female.
Reproductive system – two testicles of appropriate size for age of animal carried in a healthy scrotum. The teats should be of uniform size, showing no deviation. Any deformity or support of teats removed is will lead to the male being disqualified.

Preparation
Preparation for a goat show is very important. Make sure you have the correct licences to move your goats and make sure that they are up to date with their vaccinations – you may run a clean holding, but you don't know where the other goats are coming from.
Your goat needs to be calm and very patient. You can practice standing your goat in the correct position – the front feet directly below the shoulders and the back feet slightly apart and back – to get your goat used to the conditions of show.

Make sure you know your goat well enough to read their signals. They will let you know if they are unhappy, and if you can correct this before judging time – whether by feeding or with massage, then your goat will be a lot more comfortable and you'll have better chances.
Brush your goat's coat regularly and try to keep them in good general condition all year round to avoid any unexpected problems.

Keep the feet trimmed and the udders clean.

Judges are looking for goats of the right shape and markings for the breed standards, but also for health and wellbeing. A Boer goat that looks like they've not been well cared for is not going to win anything.

Chapter 13) Goats, the law and insurance

Before you get your Boer goat, you need to know where you stand with the law and licensing. There is no point laying out all the time, money and effort involved in starting out with these animals, bonding with them, etc, only to discover that you're breaking the law. You could risk having the animals removed and loosing your initial outlay to boot. You could even end up with a fine and a criminal record.

1. What licences do you need in your country?

UK
You currently do not need a licence to own or breed Boer goats in the UK.
If you are keeping goats on your own land it needs to be registered. You need a County Parish Holding number (CPH) to keep agricultural animals, and even if they are miniature, goats are still counted as agricultural animals.
You need to check with your house deed to make sure you are able to keep livestock, if you are keeping them in your garden.

USA
In the USA it varies from state to state as to whether or not you need a licence to keep or move your goats. You also need specific licences to move livestock between different states.

Australia
In Australia you need a licence and you are legally responsible for keeping them under control. Feral goats can cause all sorts of damage to the native flora and fauna caused by feral and escaped domestic goats. You need to prove that you can keep your animals under control.

New Zealand
As with Australia, New Zealand takes feral goats very seriously and you have a huge responsibility for your goats; you need a licence and you are legally responsible for making sure that your goats cannot get out and cause damage.

2. What are your legal responsibilities?

UK
Under the animal welfare act 2006, owners of goats in England and Wales are legally required to take reasonable steps to ensure the welfare of their animals.
Under UK law, you are responsible for the health and well being of your animal. You are responsible for the nutritional needs of your animal.
It is an offence not to provide adequate food and water.
It is an offence not to provide access to shelter.
It is an offence to allow your animal to live in unclean conditions.
It is an offence to go away without making provisions for the care of an animal.
It is an offence to intentionally harm an animal or to knowingly allow an animal to come to harm.
It is an offence not to provide adequate veterinary care.

If you are having financial difficulties this is no excuse, but the RSPCA and PDSA may be able to help out.
As goats are classed as livestock, they can't be buried or cremated by you on your land. You need to get hold of DEFRA.

USA
According to the animal welfare act of 1996, owners have legal responsibilities to their animals.
It is an offence to allow an animal to remain in pain.
It is an offence to deny, purposefully or by omission, access to adequate food and water.
It is an offence to cause pain or distress or allow pain or distress

to be caused.

You must comply with humane end points. (Humane endpoints are chosen to minimize or terminate the pain or distress of the experimental animals via euthanasia rather than waiting for their deaths as the endpoint.) Because goats are agricultural animals- even if you keep them as pets – agricultural laws should be applied to them. If your goat dies unexpectedly, you need to inform the authorities. In the USA, it is permissible to dispose of goats by burial or incineration, depending on individual state law. Contact the Department of Agriculture for state specific rules on disposal.

Chapter 14) Cost

With goats, as with any animal, there is an economy of scale in their husbandry, and the more animals you have, the less the animals cost to keep per animal. Many people feel the commitment of milking a goat or a cow is too great, but some feel they can keep a dairy animal. Land availability will often preclude the keeping of a cow and this is where the dairy goat finds her niche.

Assuming your goat never has access to grass and hedgerows and that you are not providing fresh green food, we will look at the worst case scenario of having to buy everything from a supplier. This is a broad spectrum estimate as there will always be variations on the theme, such as whether or not the goat is in milk, in kid, feeding kids and providing house milk and so on, but we will look at this in depth in a subsequent chapter.

You will need:

20kgs of good hay or a mix of 2/3 hay, 1/3 barley or oat straw per week. £3-£5, or $5-$9

Between 5 and 10kgs of proprietary goat mix per week will cost roughly £3-4, or $5-$7

One bale of bedding straw £1.50-£2 or $2-$4. Total cost £7.50 - £9 or $12-$14 per week.

If it is summer, with grazing this will be reduced dramatically, likewise if you are prepared to pick greenstuffs for your goat/s. For example, if you have a dog to walk, you might as well take a bag to collect edible weeds in for your goat, such as dandelions. A lot will depend on your circumstances.

Fencing will not be a one off cost. Goats destroy fencing. When you work out the cost of the fencing you'll be using, which will be £60-£300 or $100-$500, you should remember put something aside for repairs.

Depending on where you get your goat and what type of goat you get, your initial outlay on the animal itself will be £50-£300 or $80 -$500. A doe with a kid at foot will cost more than one who hasn't got any milk, though some people prefer to get their goat used to them before they use the goat to milk. A pedigree Boer will cost more than a cross, even though a cross could be what you really want.

Keeping Boers will cost between £600 and £1,000 or $1000 - $1500 a year per animal if they are kept without pasture. If kept with pasture, they will cost £400-£700 or $550 - $1100 a year. Depending on how many you keep, with a large herd costing less per animal.

Every 5 years or so you will need to redo the fencing too. Before all this, you'll have bought your goat too, even if you breed from your goat you will have bought some of your goats.

If your first Boer lives for 15 years and you have a small herd kept off pasture, you could end up paying £16,000 or $30,000 in total for their keep.

Kept on pasture, a Boer in a small herd will cost up to £12,000 or $20,000 in their lifetime.

If you have a larger herd of 6 or more and breed all your subsequent goats from your original doe they will cost up to £9000 or $15,000 in their lifetime.

If you also have pasture to keep your goats on you will end up paying much less per animal, more like £6,000 $10,000 per animal in their lifetime.

Selling some kids can make goat keeping more self-sustaining. If you plan to sell your kids, you will get a better price for them if they are full breed Boers.

Choose your dams and sires from large sibling groups of triplets or quads and feed them well during pregnancy. This will increase your chances of having more kids.

Chapter 15) Biology

Goats are split hoofed rumens that live on grassland and browse on other vegetation. They are considered to be small livestock animals, compared to bigger animals such as cattle, camels and Boers. This said, they're bigger than micro livestock such as hens, rabbits, and bees.

The goat, *Capra hircus,* was one of the first animals to be domesticated, eight to ten thousand years ago. The origins of the wild goats, *Capra aegagrus,* extend around the dry hills of the Mediterranean basin, including Turkey, Iran and Pakistan.

They are primarily prey animals and large predators all over the world will have a go at eating goats.

Each recognized breed of goats has specific weight ranges, which vary from over 300 lbs for bucks of larger breeds such as the Boer, to 45 to 60 lbs for smaller goat does. Within each breed, different strains or bloodlines may have different recognized sizes. At the bottom of the size range are miniature breeds such as the African Pigmy, which stand at 16 to 23 inches at the shoulder as adults.

Feral goats are most common on rocky or hilly country in the semi-arid rangelands. These areas provide security from predators and disturbance by humans. Goats are not normally found on flat, treeless plains, but can be found on flat country with dense shrub cover.

Favourable habitat requires availability of shelter, surface water and an abundance of preferred food species.

In drier districts, all sexually mature females in a herd may come into oestrus at the same time and it is thought that this is synchronised by male sexual activity. This can reduce the effects of predation by having a glut of potential victims in the form of young kids all of the same age.

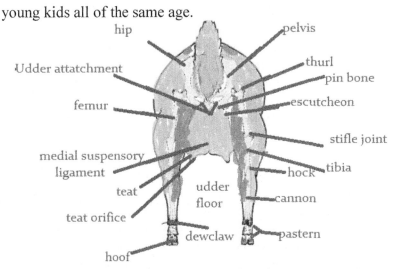

Females can begin breeding at 6 months of age or when they weigh over 15 kg. Males reach sexual maturity at approximately 8 months, but competition for access to oestrus females is fierce and it is unlikely that young males are able to mate until they become large, dominant individuals.

Females may become pregnant in their first year and can become pregnant again soon after giving birth, as lactation does not stop oestrus or pregnancy. Therefore, they can breed twice in a year, as their usual gestation period is only 150 days. Twins and triplets are common, although it is very rare for all three triplets to be raised to independence. At any time in the high rainfall zone, between 16 and 53% of females have kids at foot. The average litter size is 1.3 kids per female.

Goats reach puberty between three and 15 months of age, depending on breed and nutritional status. Many breeders prefer to postpone breeding until the doe has reached 70% of the adult weight. However, this separation is rarely possible in extensively managed, open-range herds.
In temperate climates and among the Swiss breeds, the breeding season commences as the day length shortens, and ends in early

spring or before. In equatorial regions, goats are able to breed at any time of the year. Successful breeding in these regions depends more on available forage than on day length. Does of any breed or region come into oestrus (heat) every 21 days for two to 48 hours. A doe in heat typically flags (vigorously wags) her tail often, stays near the buck if one is present, becomes more vocal, and may also show a decrease in appetite and milk production for the duration of the heat.

The intact males of many breeds come into rut in the fall, in sync with the does' heat cycles. Bucks of equatorial breeds may show seasonal reduced fertility, but as with the does, are capable of breeding at all times. Rut is characterized by a decrease in appetite and obsessive interest in the does. Sebaceous scent glands at the base of the horns add to the male goat's odour, which is important to make him attractive to the female.
In addition to natural mating, artificial insemination has gained popularity among goat breeders, as it allows easy access to a wide variety of bloodlines.

Gestation length is approximately 150 days. Twins are the usual result, with single and triplet births also common. Less frequent are litters of quadruplet, quintuplet, and even sextuplet kids. Birthing, known as kidding, generally occurs uneventfully. Just before kidding, the doe will have a sunken area around the tail and hip, as well as heavy breathing. She may have a worried look, become restless and display great affection for her keeper. The mother often eats the placenta, which gives her much-needed nutrients, helps stanch her bleeding, and parallels the behaviour of wild herbivores, such as deer, to reduce the lure of the birth scent for predators.

Freshening (coming into milk production) occurs at kidding. On average, a good quality dairy doe will give at least 6 lb (2.7 l) of milk per day while she is in milk. A first-time milker may produce less, or as much as 16 lb (7.3 l), or more of milk in exceptional cases. After the lactation, the doe will "dry off", typically after she has been bred. Occasionally, goats that have not been bred and are continuously milked will continue lactation beyond the typical 305 days.

Females that are about to give birth leave the group and give birth in a protected spot. Kids are fully active soon after birth, but most, although not all, are hidden by their mothers and visited only for feeding. A few days after birth, they join the mother on her travels. Females may then remain separate from herds containing adult males for 1 to 2 months.

The mortality rate of kids from birth to 6 months is high. Natural mortality rates amongst older goats are unknown but assumed to be about 10%. Adult mortality rates, from all causes including hunting and harvesting, are about 26% in temperate regions. Wild dogs, foxes, wedge-tailed eagles and feral pigs are all predators of feral goats. Wild dogs are the main predators of adult goats and appear to affect feral goat distribution. In northern Australia, goats are rarely present unless wild dogs are absent or controlled to low densities. Foxes are the main predators of feral goat kids in eastern Australia.

Goat populations can rapidly replenish after vigorous control programs. High levels of removal of feral goats from a population may increase survival rates and result in a faster than normal rate of increase. Goats have the potential to double their population every 1.6 years in the absence of mortality caused by human control efforts and predation.

The increased demand for goat meat, especially in the United States, could possibly be met in part through improving reproductive efficiency in our herds. Reproduction efficiency is one of the most important economic traits in terms of livestock production. Maintaining good reproductive functions in the herd is pivotal to the success of any livestock production system.

Productivity and profitability is measured by ovulation rate, conception rate, the number of kids born, the number of kids weaned and the frequency at which they are produced.
Aside from sampling many things, goats are quite particular in what they actually consume, preferring to browse on the tips of woody shrubs and trees, as well as the occasional broad-leaved plant. However, it can fairly be said that their plant diet is extremely varied, and includes some species that are otherwise toxic. They will seldom consume soiled food or contaminated water unless facing starvation. This is one reason goat-rearing is most often free ranging, since stall-fed goat rearing involves extensive upkeep and is seldom commercially viable.

Goats prefer to browse on vines, on shrubbery and on weeds, more like deer than sheep, preferring them to grasses. Nightshade is poisonous; wilted fruit tree leaves can also kill goats. Silage (fermented corn stalks) and haylage (fermented grass hay) can be used if consumed immediately after opening - goats are particularly sensitive to *Listeria* bacteria that can grow in fermented feeds. Alfalfa, a high-protein plant, is widely fed as hay; fescue is the least palatable and least nutritious hay. Goats should not be fed grass showing any signs of mould.

The digestive physiology of a very young kid (like the young of other ruminants) is essentially the same as that of a monogastric animal. Milk digestion begins in the abomasums, the milk having bypassed the rumen via closure of the reticuloesophageal groove during suckling. At birth, the rumen is undeveloped, but as the kid begins to consume solid feed, the rumen soon increases in size and in its capacity to absorb nutrients.

The adult size of a particular goat is a product of its breed (genetic potential) and its diet while growing (nutritional potential.) As with all livestock, increased protein diets (10 to 14%) and sufficient calories during the pre-puberty period yield higher growth rates and larger eventual size than lower protein rates and limited calories. Large-framed goats, with a greater skeletal size, reach mature weight at a later age (36 to 42 months) than small-framed goats (18 to 24 months) if both are fed to their full potential. Large-framed goats need more calories than small-framed goats for maintenance of daily functions. This means that Boers need more food than larger goats.

Chapter 16) Conclusion

So, now you have all the information you need to get started with raising, breeding, housing, milking, training, diet and daily care of your new pet. They really are lovely pets and make a great addition to your home or existing herd of animals. The final chapter is a list of useful websites and forums where you can find extra information on buying and caring for your Boer goat, as well as talk to experienced and enthusiastic goat owners who will hopefully be willing to help you along the way.

Don't forget that caring for your Boer goat is a legal responsibility and that it is up to you to provide adequate care, food and shelter for them. It can be a lot of work but I can assure you it is all worth it in the end, as not only are they great companions, but their milk is a great addition to any diet or food recipe.

I would like to wish you good luck if you decide to buy a Boer goat, and thank you for reading my book.

Forums and other sources of information

Forums and further info
http://www.goatbiology.com
http://www.thegoatspot.net
http://www.dairygoatforum.com
http://www.goattalk.com
http://www.dairygoatinfo.com
http://www.Boergoatclub.org
http://britishboergoatsociety.co.uk
http://crazygoatlady.com
http://www.floppyearfarm.com
http://www.homesteadingtoday.com

Feed suppliers
UK
http://www.millbryhill.co.uk
http://www.gjwtitmuss.co.uk
http://www.ebay.co.uk

USA
http://goat.purinamills.com
http://www.hiprofeeds.com
http://ebay.com
videos (information and entertainment)
http://www.youtube.com/watch?v=J3fxgi7F_qI

Buying Boer goats
USA
http://amberwavesBoergoats.com

UK
http://www.farmingads.co.uk
http://www.westonhallfarm.co.uk/

Published by IMB Publishing 2014

CPSIA information can be obtained
at www.ICGtesting.com
Printed in the USA
BVOW10s1342301117
501454BV00007B/322/P